s i m a n
m e d i a
w o r k s

BOY OF BONE

twelve stories inspired by the mütter museum

K.R. SANDS

Illustrations by

JON LEZINSKY

siman
media
works

This is a work of fiction. All of the characters and events portrayed in this work are either the products of the author's imagination or are used fictitiously.

Stories in this collection originally appeared, in slightly different versions, in the following publications: "Madame Sunday's Horn" in *Wanderings;* "What Is Written, Sweet Sister?" in *Prick of the Spindle;* "Half Life" in *Camera Obscura;* "The Face Phantom" in *Fringe Magazine;* "Leper Arrested in Ice Cream Scam" in *Rougarou;* "Do Not Feed" in *EarthSpeak;* "Mother Love" in *Milk Money* and (as "Tsantsa") in *Literary Mama;* "The Pump Twin" in *Inkspill Magazine, Joyland,* and *ShatterColors Literary Review;* and "Boy of Bone" in *The Tangled Bank: Love, Wonder, and Evolution.*

The versions of Poe's "Ulalume," "Alone," and "A Dream Within a Dream" that are excerpted in "What Is Written, Sweet Sister?" are from www.online-literature.com/poe.

Published by Siman Media Works
419 Lafayette Street, 2nd floor
New York, New York 10003
www.simanmediaworks.com

Art direction and book design by Jason Snyder
Creative Director: Benjamin Alfonsi
Production Manager: Meghan Day Healey

ISBN 978-0-9835827-2-4
Special Edition: ISBN 978-0-9835827-3-1

Color separations by Graphic Process, Inc.
www.graphicprocess.com

Printed in the United States by Worzalla
www.worzalla.com

Distributed in the United States and Canada by
Innovative Logistics
575 Prospect Street
Lakewood, New Jersey 08701
866-289-2088
www.innlog.net

To the memory of
Dr. Thomas Dent Mütter,
founder of the Mütter Museum
of the College of Physicians of Philadelphia;

and to the memory of
Harry Raymond Eastlack and the other body donors
whose deaths have given life to Dr. Mütter's museum;

and to the memory of
John Stuart Davis, my brother,
who did not live to read all these stories
but who wanted me to keep writing them.

CONTENTS

FOREWORD: HER DARK MATERIALS

ESTRAGON: All the dead voices.

VLADIMIR: They make a noise like wings.

ESTRAGON: Like leaves.

VLADIMIR: Like sand.

ESTRAGON: Like leaves.

(Silence)

VLADIMIR: They all speak at once.

ESTRAGON: Each one to itself.

(Silence)

VLADIMIR: Rather they whisper.

ESTRAGON: They rustle.

VLADIMIR: They murmur.

ESTRAGON: They rustle.

(Silence)

VLADIMIR: What do they say?

ESTRAGON: They talk about their lives.

—Samuel Beckett, *Waiting for Godot,* Act II

EVERY MUSEUM CURATOR KNOWS that the objects talk about their lives. In a medical museum, the objects—human bodies—whisper, rustle, and murmur, but their words are inaudible.

This is intentional. Medical museums are human cemeteries, and museum visitors are sensitive about their dead. Prohibited from disclosing most personal data, medical museums do not usually identify their human remains to the public. Simon Chaplin, former director of the Hunterian Museum, Royal College of Surgeons of England, comments on the anonymity of the pathological specimen: "Its accompanying case history may lay bare the most intimate details—reveal age and gender, health and habits, dissect a life with the same dispassion that has been brought to bear on the body—but the narrative is always impersonal, the patient is not named, and their voice has no place."[1] But this collection of stories by K. R. Sands is deeply personal, pointing to the undeniable need of the living to give voice to the voiceless dead.

Most of these stories belong to the genre of the "pathological sublime." Philosopher Edmund Burke posited the idea that the strongest human emotion is the experience of sublimity, which he defines as "that state of the soul in which all its motions are suspended with some degree of horror." This is surely the state of Marianne's soul in "The Jesus Wound" when she sees her husband literally crucified by surgery. And it is the state of our souls when we witness the final scene in "Mother Love," in which incestuous sexual abuse transforms a shrunken human head into a sacrificial offering. But sublimity contains elements of pleasure as well as pain. We see this pleasure in "Madame Sunday's Horn," in which the horned protagonist experiences an exquisite realization of divinity in her own resemblance to a unicorn.

Other stories involve no pathology or grotesque qualities but still nod toward Burke's idea. For instance, "Half Life" offers a playful conversation during which nothing physical occurs other than cigarette smoking. But that conversation between middle-aged Marie Curie and a mysterious young stranger concerns a study of the sublime, Marcel Duchamp's great glass picture, *The Bride Stripped Bare by Her Bachelors, Even*.

1 "Emotion and Identity in John Hunter's Museum," in Karen Ingham, ed. *Narrative Remains* (London: Hunterian Museum, Royal College of Surgeons of England, 2009:8).

And some of the stories also fit into another genre, the "humanitarian narrative," a label coined by historian Thomas W. Lacqueur. This mode of narrative depicts moral dilemmas through intense clinical descriptions of protagonists' bodily sensations, diseases, or disabilities, and their medical treatment. The radical surgery in "The Pump Twin" confronts the reader with startling implications for the definition of selfhood. Similarly, "What Is Written, Sweet Sister?" uses the savagery of the Civil War to justify a taboo-breaking act of love.

And all the stories imagine the unimaginable. Joys and terrors surface in the tangible and plausible lives of people surviving with badges of isolation, both the unusual (rare illnesses, congenital aberrations, abnormal psychologies) and the usual (death, disappointment, deprivation). We are drawn to precarious and threatening what-ifs.

The muse of K. R. Sands may be John Milton, himself blind and therefore forced to negotiate the world in ways similar to these characters. In *Paradise Lost*, Milton conjures a cosmic storm of immense energy that furnishes the Almighty with "His dark materials" to create the universe. Sands shapes the dark materials of mortality—an assemblage of grief, pleasure, and terror—into characters whose experiences take shape in the shadowy margins. We cannot *not* look. And from those margins, their voices whisper, rustle, and murmur. They talk about their lives.

Robert D. Hicks, Ph.D., Director
Mütter Museum of the College of Physicians of Philadelphia

If the dead were alive only in this world, you would forget them, looks like, as soon as they die. But you remember them, because they always were living in the other, bigger world while they lived in this little one, and this one and the other one are the same. You can't see this with your eyes looking straight ahead. It's with your side vision, so to speak, that you see it. The longer I live, and the better acquainted I am among the dead, the better I see it. I am telling what I know.

–Wendell Berry, "Stand by Me"

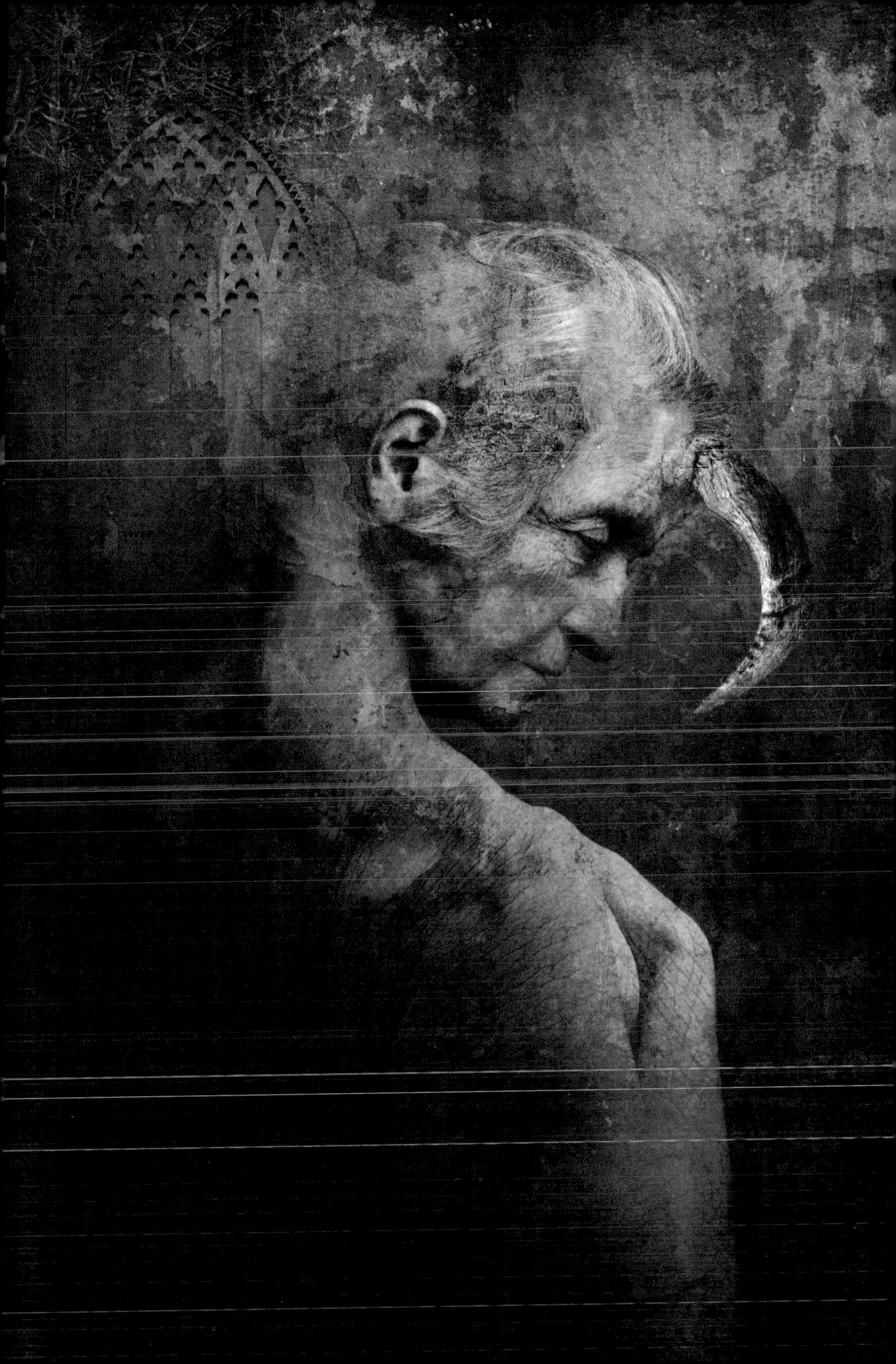

MADAME SUNDAY'S HORN

Paris, 1835

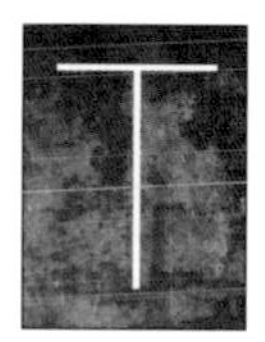

his latest horn was Madame Sunday's third.

Already an old woman when the first horn began to grow, Madame Sunday earned her living in Paris by sewing for others. She didn't do fancy tailoring, just basic cutting and stitching of necessary things like plain linen baby clothes and children's pinafores. A childless widow, she earned enough to cover her few needs. Sometimes she even had enough to buy herself a pipe of tobacco. Her life was small, but it was hers.

Her first horn—a tiny one—had grown from her left thumb, alarming her and slowing down her work. Her thread caught on the horn with every stitch, and she had to stop sewing to unwind it. She had asked Monsieur Echard, the neighborhood surgeon, to remove it, and he had complied, keeping the specimen as payment. Now, when she walked past his shop, she smiled to see her thumb-horn displayed in his front window along with the other curiosities he had acquired during the course of his work: an amputated finger on which there was a mole shaped vaguely like the head of King Charles IX, the excised cancerous eyeball of a Chinese man (acquired during Monsieur Echard's time in Canton), and several

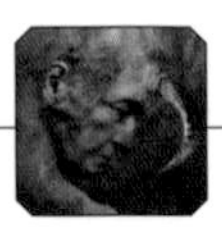

benign tumors from the scalp of an old man. These tumors were the same shape, size, and color as brown chicken eggs. Monsieur Echard said that when they had been attached to the old man's head with his sparse, twig-colored hair wrapped around them, they appeared to be snuggled in a nest. These oddities and Madame Sunday's horn now took the sun in alcohol-filled glass jars in the surgeon's shop window.

A few years after Madame Sunday had her thumb-horn removed, she noticed a second horn beginning to grow from her left cheek. Experienced now in horn-growing, she was less alarmed than she had been the first time. Besides, a horn growing from her cheek did not interfere with her work. Never a vain woman (and certainly not now, seventy-six years old and with most of her hair gone), she coexisted peacefully with the second horn for a couple of years.

Some of her neighbors and customers were initially surprised by this horn, but they soon lost interest. They had more important things to worry about than Madame Sunday's left cheek (and most of them were nothing much to look at, either). And when young boys giggled and pointed and yelled "Old Horny Witch!" from across the street, she smiled and waved.

She allowed this second horn to grow until it was the size of her little finger. When she finally decided it was time for the horn to go, she didn't bother visiting Monsieur Echard again. She knew from his removal of her first horn that there would be not much blood or pain, so she just sawed off the second horn with a kitchen knife and threw it away. The wound healed over the next few months, leaving her with a shallow scarred dent in her cheek, nothing for an old woman to worry about.

One morning a few months after Madame Sunday removed her cheek-horn, she noticed a slight protuberance in the middle of her forehead, just below her hairline. Sighing, she adjusted her linen day-cap a bit lower to cover the bump. She'd think about this new horn later. Right now she was too busy. This afternoon a customer—her own priest!—was arriving to discuss some work from her, so she bustled about her small

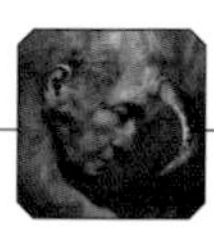

room, scouring and dusting and straightening and brewing in preparation for her guest. As she worked, she thought about the new commission. Père Goriot had told her that some valuable old tapestries had been bequeathed to the parish, but they needed repair. Madame Sunday had rarely done fancy work before, and she was apprehensive about using unfamiliar threads of silk and gold, but she was reluctant to say no to a paying job (or to her priest). She'd look at the job and then decide.

She smelled the tapestry before she saw it. As the priest unrolled it onto her work table, it gave off a strong musty odor, a scent of smoke, dust, damp, and time. Her face tightened as she thought of her morning's cleaning, and she took a step back.

But then she saw. A field of blue-green summer, rolling on forever. In the distance a ship sitting straight up on a dark blue sea, scarlet pennant whipping and pregnant sail bellying in the wind. A castle, not ruined and roofless as in Madame Sunday's time, but proud under a golden embroidered sun. Groves of trees loaded with impossibly huge fruits in apple green and lemon yellow. Among the trees, hundreds of squarish flowers that she could identify as carnations, violets, and foxgloves. Among the flowers, little people in old-fashioned outfits with preposterous hats, men and women, walking and sitting, eating and playing musical instruments, nobody laboring, nobody old.

And in the foreground, resting within a low wattle fence, the unicorn. Three of the beast's slender legs folded under its cloud-colored body, with one foreleg extended elegantly, displaying a cloven hoof. The unicorn's powerful horse-neck supported a surprisingly small head that turned its golden eyes to meet Madame Sunday's. The horn rose from just beneath its forelock, spiraling toward heaven, each turning of its ivory length delineated with filaments of shining gold, rich gold, God's gold.

Madame Sunday adjusted her cap over her forehead and her horn. She had never seen such fine stitching, such lush colors, such a spotless world. But all she said to Père Goriot was, "I think you mentioned six tapestries? Does each one have a unicorn?"

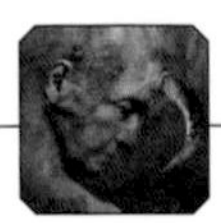

"Oh, yes," he answered. "Saint Honorius tells us that of all animals the unicorn best represents Christ: fierce yet good, selfless yet solitary. His invincible strength is represented by his horn, which defeats all evil."

Madame Sunday silently observed the unicorn.

Later, over tea, they agreed that she would take on the repair of the six tapestries. The job would be slow and arduous, but, as Père Goriot said, the finished work would redound to the glory of God. And Madame Sunday would be paid well.

Over the next six years, she allowed her other customers to slip away, putting all her skill and industry into repairing the tapestries. Père Goriot visited her occasionally to see how the work was coming along and to chat.

The old woman looked forward to these visits. She enjoyed having someone for whom she could clean, bake, and put on her best day-cap. She had liked this priest from the moment they met, in the way that a dusty old person likes a shiny new person—as a reminder of the shine under the dust. She enjoyed his animation, his long-fingered hands that fluttered like birds as he talked, the pink that flushed his cheeks, his boyish gratitude for the tea and beignets she made for him. She enjoyed his musical voice, so expressive and resonant in her usually silent room.

But he was very young. He might have been her grandson. She sometimes felt a bit silly calling him "Father."

The priest's talk was often about unicorns. He recited from Psalm 77: "And God built his sanctuary as of unicorns, in the land which he founded forever." He also explained Tertullian's idea that God intended the unicorn's horn to remind Christians of the upright stake of the crucifix, which bears Christ away from earth to heaven. He pointed to the ship on the first tapestry and said, "That mast, which represents Christ's cross, is called the unicorn mast."

While Père Goriot talked and Madame Sunday sewed, the horn on her forehead continued to grow. Over the years it grew down past her chin but remained flexible, so she was able to coil it neatly under her

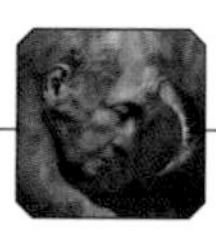

cap. She even sewed pockets into her day-caps and night-caps to contain it more securely. She artfully designed these caps to disguise the bulge made by the horn. Although she hadn't been self-conscious about her two previous horns or about the ridicule of the neighborhood children, this situation was different. Père Goriot's opinion was more important than that of the children: He was God's representative on earth. His perspective was supposed to be God's perspective. But was it really? And was she ready for God's perspective on her horn?

The problem was this: Unicorn horns were all well and good, but she wasn't a unicorn. Unicorns were supposed to have horns; people weren't. So what did hers mean? Was she possessed by a demon? Was it the mark of Cain? Was she truly a witch, as the neighborhood children teasingly said? Was the horn a sign of God's displeasure? Yes, she could go ahead and have it removed like the last two, but that wouldn't answer the underlying question. She didn't *feel* evil, but she knew her opinion on the matter was not authoritative. Probably many evil people thought themselves fine folks.

On the other hand, the horn could be a test, a sign of God's confidence in her, like Job's boils or Daniel's lions. If God kept insisting that she have horns, who was she to say no? Having it removed could be like spitting in God's face. "No, thanks, Your Highness" (or however you addressed God—she'd figure that out later), "I don't want your mark of favor. I'm happy to look like all the other sinners." Such disrespect!

What to do? She might have been able to broach the subject with a more mature, experienced priest. Her former confessor, the Abbé Desbois, had been a tough old soldier. He had fought on the side of the revolutionaries in America and France, had barely survived imprisonment and torture in the Bastille, and had cheered the beheadings of the traitors Louis XVI and Marie Antoinette. Only after the death of that dog Robespierre and the end of the Reign of Terror had he finally put away his arms and taken the cloth. And he had had plenty of women along the way. Yes, that old man had seen it all. He knew about the world and about

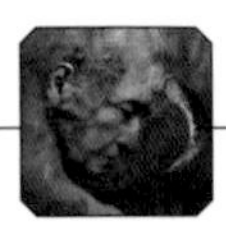

sin. He wouldn't have batted an eye if Madame Sunday had bristled with horns all over. His rough good sense would have been a comfort to her, but he had died years ago.

Père Goriot was another matter. Young, fresh, smooth-faced, innocent—a boy, really—he still lived in Eden. What did he know of sin or evil? Madame Sunday would have staked her horn that he had never seen any woman naked. Certainly he had never fought any battles or seen the inside of a prison. Trained for the priesthood from youth, he had a scholar's pale skin and ink-stained fingers. Whereas the Abbé Desbois had been good at listening, Père Goriot was good at talking. His musical voice, his vast knowledge of Scripture, his visionary imagination—she loved to hear him speak of beautiful things: of Christ's crimson blood, of the Virgin's sky-blue cloak, of shining unicorns, of the golden glory of God when she would at last stand in his presence.

But as the six years passed and she realized ever more keenly that she was coming nearer to that presence, she felt increasingly worried. What would God see when he looked at her horn? She wanted to ask Père Goriot for the answer, but she wished there were some way for her to know the answer before she asked. Since this wasn't possible, she kept quiet.

When the work was finished and Père Goriot had taken away the tapestries and no longer visited Madame Sunday, she felt restless and empty. She decided to call on Monsieur Echard, whom she had not seen in a long time.

Approaching his surgeon's shop, she noticed a new specimen in the window, an amazing thing in a glass jar: a human infant girl with two heads! Putting her face as close as she could to the glass, Madame Sunday inspected this marvel: diminutive, perfect nails on the toes and fingers; creases like bracelets around the wrists and ankles; and pale, wispy hair on both heads. The brownish-red stump of the umbilical cord protruded from the belly. Perhaps not as beautiful as a unicorn, but just as astonishing.

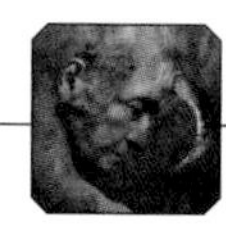

After entering the shop and greeting Monsieur Echard, she asked him about the new specimen.

He laughed and said, "Oh, it's not real. It's a *moulage*, a wax model made to educate medical students who do not have access to the real specimen in the collection of the Musée Dupuytren. This model duplicates the real specimen in every detail. It was created by Europe's most renowned wax modeler, Monsieur Jules Baretta, who lives here in Paris. I was lucky enough to get one of his models only because he is an acquaintance of mine."

Madame Sunday was amazed to hear that the specimen that she had seen as flesh was actually wax. After thinking a moment, she was also delighted. To her friend she said, "I would like to show you something."

In Monsieur Baretta's modeling studio, Madame Sunday removed her day-cap to free her horn for inspection. She allowed her neck to be clamped to the high back of a wooden chair and her wrists to be clamped to the chair's arms. In this uncomfortable position, she watched the face of the master modeler as he measured, felt, and sketched. He gauged the horn several times to make sure of his accuracy: Yes, it was indeed 24.9 centimeters long. Under his breath he muttered, "A magnificent *cornu cutaneum*, the grandest ever seen." Madame Sunday warmed to the compliment.

Monsieur Baretta continued to mumble as he made his notations: "Horn too thick to encircle with thumb and forefinger . . . lengthwise striations, as if raked repeatedly with a fork . . . the tip opaque amber, remainder brownish-black." As he made his inspection, his face came so close to Madame Sunday's that his two eyes merged into one giant eye that hovered just in front of her horn. His sour breath caused her to flinch, and he said, "Be still, please. I won't be much longer." Madame

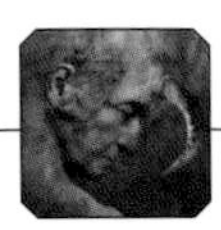

Sunday closed her eyes and breathed calmly. A unicorn was superior to a cyclops.

When she was released from bondage, Madame Sunday asked to look at the sketches. The master complied, warning her that they were incomplete. She was surprised to see, not her face and horn, but just graphite slashes of planes, angles, shadings, and numbers. The master said that he would complete the drawings and create the wax model later.

To Madame Sunday's question about where the finished model would reside, Monsieur Baretta said, "I have already arranged to donate it to the Musée Dupuytren, where dozens of distinguished physicians and surgeons and medical students will see it daily as they pass along the grand corridors of the museum. The model of your face and horn will speak to the educated and the ignorant, the learners and the gapers. Thousands of people will admire it in the centuries to come."

Madame Sunday thought about admiration. She had lately seen some wonders.

When the important day arrived, Monsieur Baretta called for her in his fashionable new curricle, and they drove to the museum. Before he showed her the wax model of her face, however, he wanted her to see some of his other creations. She suppressed her impatience as he escorted her into a room with dark green moiré walls and glass-fronted mahogany display cases holding the master's smaller models. Madame Sunday looked as Monsieur Baretta spoke: "Here is a set of four aspects of the female breast in advancing stages of cancer. Here are three specimens showing the female mammary gland after the removal of the skin. And here is a specimen showing the milk ducts of the female mammary gland."

The wax breasts sat as snugly as eggs inside their cozy nests of ruffled white silk. The edges of the nests were bound in scarlet braid to keep them from fraying. Madame Sunday automatically noticed the fine

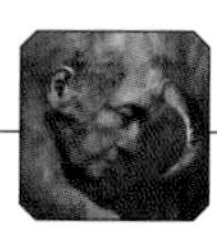

stitching on the braid, but her mind also registered something more surprising: Rather than being disturbed by the disembodied wax breasts, as she would have expected, she found herself admiring the care and craftsmanship that had gone into their creation.

Monsieur Baretta then showed Madame Sunday twenty wax models of human embryos in various stages of development up to the third month of pregnancy. These models were far tinier than the smallest of the old woman's fingers, tinier even than the smallest of her horns. They lay, like the wax breasts, curled inside ruffled white nests, looking like sleeping goblins, all pointy ears and secret smiles. Madame Sunday's response again surprised her, as she found herself admiring Monsieur Baretta's artistry. After all, the objects before her were not really human embryos—that was just their disguise. But she could see them for what they were: man's creations in imitation of God's.

Next, Monsieur Baretta wanted to show Madame Sunday one of the large wax models that lay on a polished walnut table in the middle of the room. As he gently lifted a white silk cover, he said, "Here is a female whole-body specimen showing the lymphatic vessels in the thoracic and abdominal cavities." Madame Sunday looked at a naked young woman whose entire body lay on a white silk pillow edged with dark red fringe. The woman lay on her back, right knee slightly lifted to obscure her sex, right arm bent at the elbow to touch one of the bright golden strands of hair that trailed across her shoulder. Her lovely face was turned to Madame Sunday, rosy lips parted, brown eyes open and frank. The string of pearls around her neck emphasized her nakedness, as did her shiny black wax slippers.

This model looked like any young woman welcoming a lover to her bed, except for one thing: Her chest and abdomen gaped open from the base of her throat to the bottom of her belly. Erupting from the cavity was a profusion of unfamiliar tubular shapes in dark red and brownish-yellow, each shape clutched by a network of tendrils and fronds and strands. While Monsieur Baretta was saying, "Liver . . . colon . . . stomach

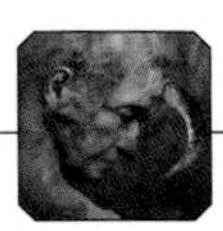

. . . blood vessels . . . lymph nodes . . . vena cava . . . aorta," Madame Sunday was mesmerized. Someone else might recoil at the young woman's exploding body, but she was awash with admiration at the beauty of the work.

Finally, Monsieur Baretta led her to a small wall-mounted case whose glass front was covered by a white silk curtain. He drew aside the curtain, and there it was: her wax face crowned with its wax horn. Madame Sunday looked in silence for a long time.

Was this also beautiful? She knew that *she* was not beautiful, but was not Monsieur Baretta's model a form of praise, of prayer, in its commemoration of God's work? Although she would probably never see Monsieur Baretta again after this day, she and he would always be connected by this model, by her horn. And although she would never meet the thousands of people who would see this horned face of wax after her face of flesh was gone, those people, too, would have a connection with her. The horn must then also join her to God, mustn't it?

As she looked, she remembered a lovely thing that Père Goriot had once said: "Did you know that a group of unicorns is called 'a blessing'? I think that's a wonderful saying: a blessing of unicorns."

So, after all, her horn had been a gift. But now that its image would live forever in wax, she no longer needed to wear it on her face. She could let Monsieur Echard remove it and display it in his shop window, taking the sun with her first horn. And she could finally go to meet God with her day-cap neat and tidy, no unsightly bulge in the front.

Eighty-four years old. Her mother had not lived half so long. She was ready.

THE JESUS WOUND

Edinburgh, 1856

arianne waited alone at Saint Giles' Cathedral. Tom would be all right without her for a few hours. The guest house proprietors would keep an eye on him. On this Tuesday morning, the High Kirk's population was mostly construction workers and tourists rather than worshippers. How strange: God's house as a common thoroughfare rather than a holy destination.

Marianne's church at home in Germantown was small and simple, with a whitewashed interior that reflected light into every corner. Sitting inside, she could track the circuit of the sun by the shifting strength of the clear light through the windows.

But this church! A dark, cold pile the size of a small town, as tunneled as a badger warren. So huge that, despite the gigantic windows all around, the crossing was dark. Vaulted arches soared overhead; Gothic tracery filled the upper walls. She sat small in the darkness, as far away as possible from the ostentation, closing her eyes and humming quietly.

Hymns had always been her comfort. The plagal cadence of each

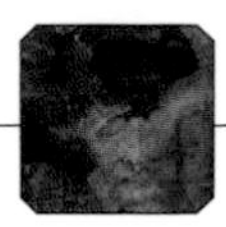

"Amen" enfolding her mind. The smoothing, purposeful, horizontal movement of the harmony. The easy changes of the chords, dissonant only momentarily, never uncomfortably so.

Alone, she routinely sang or hummed. In company, she listened to the music in her head. Melody, harmony, and rhythm she had understood for as long as she could remember. No, *understood* was the wrong word. *Known,* maybe. Or *owned.* Yes, music was what she owned. What she was allowed to own. Everything else was owned by others. Even she was owned by others: first by her mother, then by Tom, and always by Jesus.

When her mother had catechized her, saying, "What is thy only comfort in life and death?" Marianne knew the answer. It was there in her head; she could hear it: "That I with body and soul, both in life and in death, am not my own, but belong to my faithful Savior Jesus Christ, who, with his precious blood, has fully satisfied for all my sins, and delivered me from all the power of the devil." But she couldn't say it. She knew she'd stumble on the word *blood,* gag on it. It was a word too powerful to speak. So she stayed mute, tears running down her face while her mother scolded and slapped her. Afterward, sitting in penitential isolation in the dark cellar, she sang to calm her racing heart. She could hear nothing except the transmission of her voice through the bones of her head, fuller and more reverberant than when transmitted through mere air. The music felt like God's hands cupped around her.

When her father had prepared to leave for the China Inland Mission, Marianne had watched him pack his belongings, not into a trunk, but into a coffin. Even so, she had not fully understood that he would never return. But the day they learned he had died of cholera, her mother, stone-faced, had turned to her and said, "Now I will go to live with your brother. Your marriage will take place next month. The doctor will arrange everything, so you need not concern yourself." Marianne had nodded and retired to her room. She sat on the edge of her bed, looking out the open window at the fallen magnolia petals browning and rotting on the grass. Then she closed her eyes and sang.

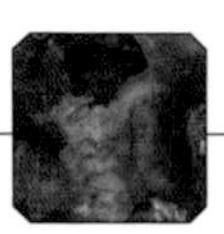

When Tom had asked her to marry him, had backed her up against the garden wall and opened his arms, she had wanted to say that she wasn't sure or that she needed to think or (even) the truth, which was that she was afraid. Of being touched by a man. Even more, of being abandoned by a man. She tried to meet Tom's gaze, but a crimson film cascaded over her mind, blinding and silencing her. So she closed her eyes and received his hands on her waist, his mouth on her mouth, her mind retreating behind the waterfall of music that slowly drowned out the sound of her dread.

The blood of the wedding night showed her the color of marriage. Tom was a surgeon, after all. Blood was his world. And she was a woman, with blood her monthly reminder of the perniciousness of all women. Of her failure, once again, to bear Tom a child. And when, a year or so after the wedding, she found Tom's handkerchief spotted with blood, she thought of her father packing his belongings into his coffin.

She began to listen more carefully to the words of her hymns. It was surprising how often the blood appeared.

Rock of Ages, cleft for me, let me hide myself in thee!
Let the water and the blood from thy riven side which flowed
Be of sin the double cure; save from wrath and make me pure.

She thought it shouldn't be "the water and the blood," but the reverse. Had not the Evangelist said that Jesus was "the one who came by blood and water," that "blood and water flowed out of the pierced side"? Or was she wrong?

One evening she had asked Tom why the blood might come before the water.

"I can't think of any medical explanation," he said. "A heavy flow of blood could be explained by the wound's being on the right side, as the paintings show, indicating the spear's perforation of the distended, thin-walled right atrium. Isn't it possible that by mentioning the blood

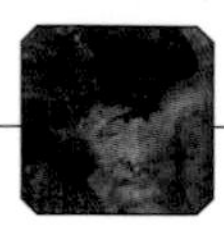

before the water, John is simply emphasizing its importance as a symbol of Christ's life?"

She countered, "But the water—symbol of the Holy Spirit—is equally important."

"Well," Tom said. "So much for my expertise in symbolism. I should stick to medicine. My best medical guess is that the word 'water' meant serous pleural and pericardial fluid that preceded, not followed, the flow of blood."

They had discussed this subject as he sat in his chair late one night, tired from work. (He arose before dawn six days a week to attend patients and give medical lectures until well after dark.) Marianne had applied a cold compress to his poor, tired eyes and lightly massaged his temples. Tom deserved a better match, she knew. He should have married a brilliant conversationalist, an educated intellectual, a skilled lover. But at this moment she felt useful to him. Wifely, not childish.

He said, "Ah, that feels wonderful. Don't stop. And sing to me."

She continued massaging. "You know my voice is not of solo quality."

"But it is the voice I love. Please."

She obeyed her husband.

O how sweet to trust in Jesus, just to trust His cleansing blood,
Just in simple faith to plunge me 'neath the healing, cleansing flood!

Agnes Lister was not the intimidating bluestocking Marianne had been fearing. When she noticed Marianne staring at the sensible rubber boots under her plain serge hem, she laughed and said, "We're in Scotland, dear. Weather trumps fashion." And when Marianne admitted to having had no breakfast, Mrs. Lister said, "We'll remedy that right now." She set her carpet-bag on the stone base of one of the columns and took out a paper twist and a small earthenware jar. When Marianne expressed discomfort about eating

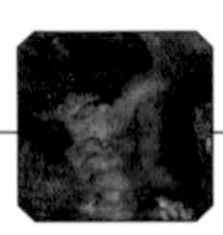

inside a church, Mrs. Lister said, "Soul and body, both must be fed. I made these bannocks and crowdie myself. Eat." At the first taste of the soft, mildly sour cheese spread generously over the sweet, crumbly oatcake, Marianne felt an immediate easing in her forehead. She was very hungry. When she politely demurred at eating a second bannock, her new friend calmly said, "Nonsense," and handed over another. Only when Mrs. Lister was satisfied that Marianne was sufficiently filled did they leave the church and walk to the Natural History Collections at the University of Edinburgh.

Now they paced slowly through the dark rooms, stopping frequently to inspect some rarity in a glass case—a squid bigger than a rowboat, a flightless bird taller than a man, a sticklike insect longer than a human hand. These displays Marianne passed with no comment. God in his infinite wisdom had created every conceivable creature to compose the great chain of being. Educated people such as Tom and the Listers were now saying that these creatures—and all others—were much older than she had been taught to believe. That they had come into being over millions of years, not all at once on the fifth and sixth days of creation. This new idea caused much confusion, doubt, excitement, argument—it hurt her head to think about it. She subdued the pain with music.

He breaks the power of canceled sin,
He sets the prisoner free;
His blood can make the foulest clean,
His blood availed for me.

But here a concatenation of irregular shapes, brightly colored like a child's toy, caught her eye. What was she looking at? The central shape on the bottom was heavy and sagging, a giant's scrotum (the word Tom would use), half blue and half red. Rising from behind, a white ringed tube like a stalk of bamboo. Alongside the tube, a pair of crimson long-necked snails, horns pricked. Most amazing of all, flanking these central shapes, two wild-branching bushes, shaped and colored like coral.

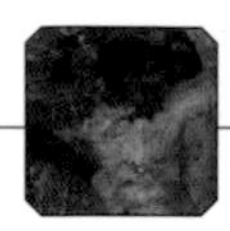

She had learned long ago not to say, "What is it?" Educated people drew back and took a breath before answering this question in the same even, indulgent voice and simple language they used with children. Much better to say, "Tell me about this," which implied familiarity but also deference to the other's superior knowledge.

Mrs. Lister answered, "Well, as you can see, it's a preserved specimen of the human heart and lungs. The lung tissue has been removed by corrosion to expose the bronchial tree. This specimen is one of the best in the world because of its completeness—you can see how full the tree is—and the vividly colored waxes differentiating the organs. Have you ever seen a specimen like this before?"

"No. Only drawings. And they never show the bronchi and alveoli as fully as this. It's beautiful, isn't it?"

Mrs. Lister smiled. Marianne was saying the right things. So the giant's scrotum was the heart, the bamboo stalk was the trachea, and the horned snails were the truncated aorta and vena cava. Yes, now it did look like the medical illustrations. But if she narrowed her eyes and took a step back, it transmogrified again into mystery. She experimented, widening and narrowing her eyes, moving herself forward and back. It was like seeing a painting at an art gallery: If she stood behind the invisible line, the illusion was perfect. But one step forward, and it shattered into a thousand brushstrokes. She preferred to stand behind the line, to be inside the mystery. Tom, of course, always took that step over, wanting to see what was behind the illusion.

She took a step forward.

Marianne sat silently as the two doctors talked. Dr. Lister had recommended that she attend the preoperative conference, and Tom had concurred. Both men thought she should learn what to expect from the surgery. Of course, she had obeyed her husband.

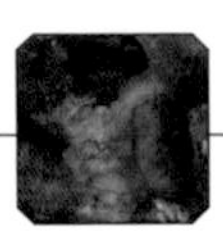

She watched, seeing Tom as Dr. Lister saw him. The two doctors had met five years earlier at an international surgical conference in Berlin. Lister had no doubt been impressed by the older man's excellent posture, the crown of copious dark curls, the arrogant Roman features, the firm step. Now Tom was gaunt and bent, with sunken eyes and whitened hair, mouth drawn down in fatigue and pain. But he still wore a beautiful silk cravat pinned with a large pearl.

Dr. Lister spoke too quickly. From assurance that Tom had the same technical vocabulary he did? From embarrassment? His listener—his patient—was his professional superior: head of an academic surgery department rather than merely an assistant hospital surgeon, as Lister was.

But Marianne knew that Tom had especially wanted to consult Dr. Lister, whom he considered the best of the next generation of physicians. Lister's mentor, the venerable Dr. Syme, and Lister's hospital, the Royal Infirmary of Edinburgh, had set the surgical standards that the rest of the world endeavored to meet. Not only an excellent surgeon, Lister was also a brilliant researcher. His preliminary experiments using carbolic acid to reduce the postoperative mortality rate had yielded promising results. Marianne had expressed some doubt that a consultation with Lister would be worth the arduous journey, but Tom was adamant.

She could see that Dr. Lister reciprocated Tom's respect. Tom, after all, was a celebrity in the European–American medical sphere. Not for his publications, few and brief. Not for his medical lectures, entertaining and lively, but other physicians could claim the same. But for his surgical skills and, especially, for his collection.

Tom had begun the collection two decades previously, when Marianne and the Listers were still children. He had visited Paris at the beginning of his career, had met Guillaume Dupuytren and other great medical men, had become fascinated by the truth and beauty of European anatomical imagery. He had taken home to Philadelphia a wax model of an old woman's face, an image showcasing the longest human horn anyone had ever seen.

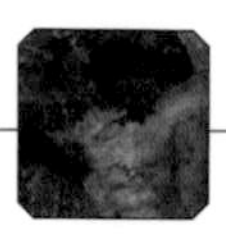

The collection grew quickly. Tom persuaded his colleagues to donate anatomical specimens from surgical operations and postmortem examinations. Bones with anchylosis, caries, deformities, and fractures. Preserved ears, noses, hands, and genitals. Abscesses and aneurysms, bladders and bullet wounds, cartilage and cancers, and on down the alphabet. He'd used his inherited wealth and European connections to commission medical paintings in watercolor and oil, anatomical models in plaster, wax, and *papier-mâché*. Now, twenty years later, he owned the world's most extensive private collection of human pathologies, more than seventeen hundred unique specimens.

Students, physicians, and surgeons traveled from all over the world to see and learn from the collection. It would be of inestimable value in their attempts to better the human condition, to rid mankind of its multitudinous plagues: smallpox, leprosy, gout, malaria, meningitis, tetanus, epilepsy, diphtheria, cholera, yellow fever, pneumonia typhoid dysentery diabetes emphysema syphilisgangrenecancer ... And perhaps Tom's own demon: consumption. Pulmonary tuberculosis. Phthisis. The white plague. Cause unknown. No effective treatment. No cure. No hope.

But, Marianne knew, the collection meant something private to Tom as well. Orphaned at two years old with no siblings, Tom had grown to adulthood under the care of headmasters and distant relations. He had no children. His only family consisted of her and the people whose body parts made up his collection.

The collection would be Tom's greatest gift to the world. It would also be his epitaph—soon. Steaming across the Atlantic from Philadelphia to Edinburgh to undergo surgery could accomplish no more than a stay of execution. Consumption followed an inexorable course, unfazed by human attempts to slow or stop it. Tom knew it. Marianne knew it. Dr. Lister knew it.

Nonetheless, convention dictated that Dr. Lister listen to Tom's summary of symptoms, offer his best diagnosis, and recommend a course of action. That action might serve no purpose other than making Tom

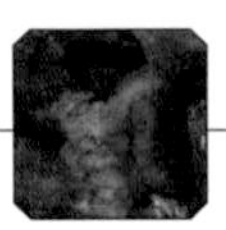

feel that he, not the disease, was still in control of his life, but that was something. In the absence of a cure, it was much.

And so Marianne listened as Dr. Lister spoke quickly. What he had to say was not new information but a necessary part of the ritual. "From your description of the chest pains and shortness of breath, I suspect a major pneumothorax, undoubtedly a consequence of the tuberculosis. I propose to insert a chest drain into the right pleural cavity. The insertion target will be the fifth intercostal space slightly anterior to the mid-axillary line. The drain will be attached to a sealed vessel below chest level. This arrangement will allow the excess air to escape from the pleural space."

Tom answered with the hoarseness of the chronic cougher. "I assume you chose the right lung because its volume and capacity exceed that of the left, making it the safer insertion site."

Marianne wondered. Why say this? To remind Lister that Tom's medical judgment was equal to his? No—this was about the patient, not the doctor. To remind himself.

"Yes, that's right. Once the tube is inserted, I'll suture it in place and affix a dressing. It can remain until the pneumothorax is sufficiently reduced to allow for the tube's removal."

"Will you place the tube with a trocar or guide wire?"

Marianne watched Dr. Lister draw back. Even she knew a trocar would be reckless. But Lister's voice was even. "Guide wire. It will take longer but greatly reduce the risk of lung puncture."

"Would it be possible for me to undergo the procedure while awake? So I can observe the work?"

Dr. Lister paused, and Marianne suppressed a smile. Yes, Tom did fancy himself a demigod in strength, sleeping only four or five hours a night, driving himself hard the rest of the time. But Lister's voice maintained its professional pitch and volume. "No. You'll need to be asleep. We've recently begun using ether—" He stopped when Tom shook his head. "Then opium in sherry. You'll be supine for the incision and the

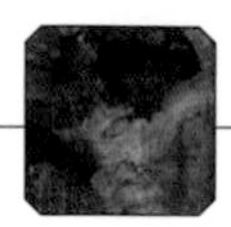

insertion of the chest drain. Once the operation is over, we'll tilt the operating table to enable gravitational assistance for the drain. You'll be snugly strapped to the table, so the tilting won't disturb you."

"What about the drainage canister? How much will it limit my mobility?"

Marianne turned to look at Tom. How mobile did he think he was going to be? He had spent almost all of his two weeks aboard ship lying in bed or blanket-wrapped in a deck chair. He had dressed and gone to supper only twice.

"The tube we're using has a shutoff valve, and the canister is small and portable. You can detach and remove the canister for walking, dressing, and so forth. Of course, I encourage you to keep it in use as much as possible."

She knew better. Tom would probably detach the canister during the return voyage and toss it over the side of the ship.

"And now I must advise you of the risks and possible complications of this procedure."

"Not necessary. I'm fully conversant with them. How soon may I remove the tube?"

She could see: Tom didn't want to hear it, but Lister had to say it.

"Dr. Mütter, you know that it is my professional responsibility to inform you of the risks and possible complications of this procedure. Serious risks include hemorrhage, pulmonary edema, and cardiac arrest. Minor risks include shortness of breath, coughing, possibly subcutaneous hematoma. Proper maintenance of the drainage tube, to keep it as open and free-flowing as possible, will help reduce these risks. Now, as to pain—"

"Oh, I have a very high tolerance for pain. That doesn't concern me. But the tube's removal—"

"Dr. Mütter." Lister's words were now developing sharper edges, his cheeks glowing pinkly. "We will be penetrating the chest wall. You will probably experience pain as long as the drain is in place. At times, the

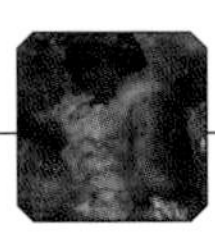

pain might be significant. If the intercostal space is scarred by the procedure, which is not uncommon, you'll need to manage chronic pain for the rest of your life, even after removal of the drain."

"Yes, the drain. That's what I wanted to talk about. How soon can I dispense with it?"

Tom hadn't heard anything Lister had said. He thought he would come out of this procedure and be the man he was five years ago. Marianne sighed. No, he didn't really think that. He only wished it.

"I'm afraid it will be several months at least. Much depends on how quickly the pneumothorax reduces and on whether it reinflates. The drain removal should not be rushed."

Not rushed? Not only would Tom throw the drainage canister into the ocean, he would probably remove his own sutures and toss the tube as well. Why were they going through this charade?

But looking at her husband's gaunt face and haunted eyes, she knew why. This would be Tom Mütter's final battle with his demon. He knew he would eventually lose, but his habit was to fight. A warrior, he repudiated the badges of weakness.

As the men's conversation continued in its ritualistic round, Marianne closed her eyes and listened to something else.

There is a fountain filled with blood drawn from Emmanuel's veins;
And sinners plunged beneath that flood lose all their guilty stains.
Lose all their guilty stains, lose all their guilty stains;
And sinners plunged beneath that flood lose all their guilty stains.

Although Marianne could have watched the operation, she chose not to. She would not shame Tom by witnessing his professional emasculation. So she sat again in the High Kirk, eyes closed, hands folded in her lap, and thought about blood.

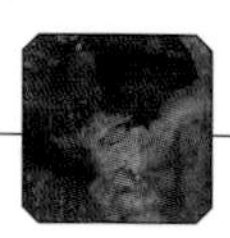

Count Zinzendorf, the spiritual founder of the Moravian community in Bethlehem, Pennsylvania, had written hymns and sermons that celebrated Jesus' side wound as the birthplace of souls. Marianne's parents had raised her to believe that the Jesus wound was a spiritual vagina, a womanly aperture. The feminizing wound accomplished Jesus' incarnation as a complete human being, both male and female, who redeemed women—in all their perniciousness—as well as men, the body as well as the soul. The first Moravian church at Bethlehem had a wall niche lined with red fabric. Into this "birthplace" were placed infants at baptism and the corpses of the dead, both reborn through Christ's vaginal wound.

The count had also said that marital coition was a sacramental celebration of the union of the soul with Christ. Marianne had thought about this idea on her bloody wedding night and on many subsequent nights. It had taken her months to move from *naming* this act a celebration to *feeling* it as one. But that feeling had been shadowed by the revelation that the childlessness of her marriage was a function of Tom's illness.

At this thought, God's hand closed around her heart, almost stopping it. She doubled over, head on knees, heaving hoarse, breathless sobs. Covering the back of her head with her clasped hands, she rocked to and fro, moaning, keening. Lamenting all the deaths—of her Tom, her husband, a good surgeon, a good man. Of her marriage, her wifehood, her chance for motherhood. Of her girlhood, her father. And, especially, the death of her trust—in parents, in children, in doctors. In God? Oh, she didn't know, she didn't know. She rocked herself as she would have rocked her child.

She felt a light touch on her shoulder. "Miss, shall I fetch the verger?"

Marianne sat up, face wet, and looked at the boy. Her brain was slow to process the strange word in the strange pronunciation. *Vair-jair.* A few tourists were staring. The boy looked about twelve, still in Eden. He would experience his expulsion soon enough.

She had to respond. Smiling to reassure the boy, she shook her head. Took her handkerchief—one of Tom's, actually, from which she had washed the blood many times—and blotted her face. Said quietly,

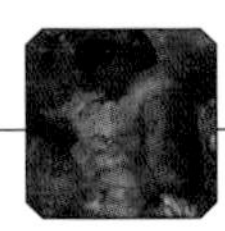

"Thank you, no. I am composed now. You are very kind." The boy looked at her uncertainly for a few more seconds, then left.

No, she still had God. The music told her so. While Tom's body was being pierced, she raised her head, closed her eyes, and listened.

Little side hole! Little side hole! Little side hole, thou art mine!
Dearest little side hole, I wish myself inside you.
Thou art my little soul, the dearest little place.
Deep inside! Deep inside! Deep inside the little side!

Marianne had forgotten that the table would be tilted to allow the chest drain to work better. She expected to see Tom lying flat, safely tucked under a sheet. But he was upright. Crucified. Showing the side wound, Jesus' mortal laceration.

Her stomach lurched; she closed her eyes against the sight.

Of the righteousness of God thro' the blood effusion,
Of that daily bread and food Thou mak'st distribution.

No. She could not resort to blindness at this moment. She must be a wife, not a child. Opening her eyes, she walked slowly forward.

It was not a cross, only a table tilted upright to an angle nearly perpendicular to the floor. Tom's ankles, waist, upper chest, and forehead were bound securely to the table with leather straps. His arms were outstretched, wrists strapped to the crossbar, chest faintly rising and falling. The wound just under his right nipple extruded a long tube that emptied into the drainage jar on the floor.

She kept walking until she stood next to her husband. She placed one hand on his thin chest, over his heart, and the other on his gaunt cheek. Then she put her mouth to his ear, delivering her music *sotto voce.*

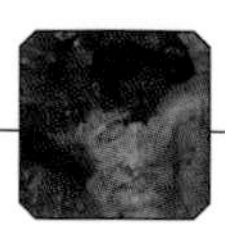

Morning Star, O cheering sight! Ere thou cam'st how dark earth's night!
Morning Star, my soul's true light, tarry not, dispel my night.

Tom's eyelids flickered.

Four days later, sitting up in bed with Mrs. Pitkethly's wool blankets tossed to the floor, Tom smiled at Marianne, catching her wrist as she walked by. "*Meine Frau! Setz dich zu mir.*"

She sat on the edge of the bed and smoothed the wild curls away from his forehead. He took her hand and kissed the palm. Then he moved his mouth to her wrist, to the inside of her forearm, and up to her inner elbow, kissing wetly and noisily all the way. She laughed while he made silly snuffling noises along her arm. Then she leaned forward. The kiss began tentatively, gently. She held the sides of his face; he held her shoulders. The kiss continued, becoming surer but never hard. Their mouths fitted together, exactly the right size for each other. The tongues. His hand trailing down the front of her shoulder to the top of her breast. The heat in her fingers, her ears. Her thighs. Her hand moving down to rest on his belly.

She whispered, "When you are better, my dear." They had not enjoyed erotic love in many months.

"Yes. When I am better."

A week after the operation, Tom dressed and came down—slowly—to supper, leaning on Mr. Pitkethly's arm. Although he didn't eat much, he complimented Mrs. Pitkethly's beef broth and hot Scotch eggs with gravy. He refrained from smoking after the meal, joking that laudanum was his new tobacco. He asked Mr. Pitkethly to favor the table with his

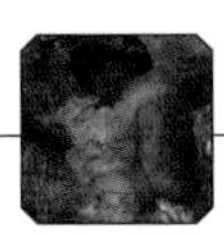

barrel-bellied rendition of Scott's "Bonnie Dundee." All the stanzas, please. As that gentleman lifted his voice, Marianne and Tom clapped in time. And they sang along to the chorus, the only part of the song they knew.

Come fill up my cup, come fill up my can,
Come saddle my horses and call out my men,
Unhook the west port and let us gae free,
For it's up wi' the bonnets o' bonnie Dundee!

So triumphant! Those nimble octave leaps like a trumpet fanfare—the music of victory. And Dundee had indeed won that decisive battle at Killiecrankie.

But he had lost his life in that same battle. Forty-one years old.

About Tom's age.

After Marianne tucked Tom into the deck chair and secured the drainage jar out of harm's way, she sat next to him. "Do you wish to sleep? Or shall I sing?"

"Both. You sing, I'll sleep. Sing that one about the spotless robe. Do you know the one I mean?"

"Yes, of course. It's Zinzendorf's. What tune? Old Hundredth or Walton?"

"Old Hundredth. All hymns should be sung to it."

She smiled and began.

Bold shall we stand in that great day,
For who aught to our charge shall lay,
While by Thy blood absolved we are
From sin and guilt, from shame and fear?

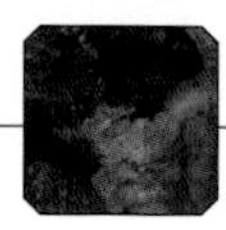

He slept almost immediately. Part of her brain continued to direct her diaphragm, throat, and mouth. Her singing voice, whatever its inadequacies, was now his reassurance as well as her own.

But another part of her brain rehearsed the list of tasks that she needed to accomplish over the next few weeks. Order the creation of a catalogue of Tom's collection. Hire a private nurse. Meet with Tom's bank officer.

She took out her stationery box and, still singing, began to write. After Tom woke, she'd have him sign the letter. She could post it as soon as they landed.

May 20, 1856

Esteemed Colleagues and Fellows
of the College of Physicians of Philadelphia

Gentlemen:

In consequence of ill health, I am obliged to resign my office as a professor of surgery. To render some return to my profession for the benefits derived from its prosecution for so many years and, above all, to serve the cause of science and humanity, I have determined to found a medical museum which shall be open to all. I herewith offer the guardianship of my collection to the College as the body best qualified by the character of its members and the nature of its pursuits for undertaking the trust. I desire the museum to receive the following designation: *Pathological Museum of the College of Physicians of Philadelphia. Founded by Thomas Dent Mütter, M.D.*

WHAT IS WRITTEN, SWEET SISTER?

Central Virginia, 1864

Spotsylvania Wilderness, May 6.

Third day of battle. Evil location: dark woods, thick scrub, rough terrain. The two armies continue to shoot breast to breast, blind in the dense rifle smoke. Dry timber caught flying sparks yesterday and burst into brushfire, spreading fast. When I first heard the eerie wail above the barrage, I didn't know what it was. Now I know: the helpless wounded, burning alive.

We're working under a tent fly to protect us from the rain that finally put that fire out. My back is turned to the drenched and wounded soldiers lying on the muddy ground. Thousands of them, a sea of men stretching as far as I could see, if I looked. I don't.

I'm packing an elbow stump with lint. The man is chloroformed and morphined, so he's no trouble. His amputated hand and lower arm crown the pile of limbs rising like Golgotha, taller than I am. I don't know how long I've been operating. Twenty-four hours? Twenty-eight? If I sit to rest for a moment, I won't be able to get up again.

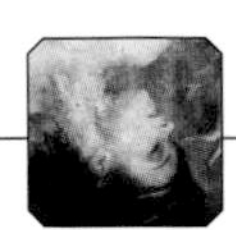

I shout Fitzpatrick's name, and someone turns to me. (We're all covered in brown-black blood, indistinguishable as demons.) "Get those limbs out of here. And while you're outside, check the waiting wounded." He knows to ignore those wounded in the head, chest, or belly; they'll die anyway. He'll be looking for those with limb wounds; they still have a chance. He shovels the amputated arms and legs into a wheelbarrow and goes.

While he's outside, she approaches me, dirty, frightened. It takes me a second to recognize her: one of the laundresses, the youngest one. Strands of red-gold hair escape from under her cap.

I've almost finished bandaging the stump. "Are you hurt? Do you need help?"

"I'm all right, sir, but please . . . my brother." She points to a man lying on the ground just inside the shade of the tent fly.

"That man?" A molten corpse. "He's beyond my help."

"No, I mean—please help me with him. I need—" She chokes.

I knot the bandage and signal a steward to get the anesthetized man off my table to make room for the next one. "What? What?" I hear the impatience in my voice, but I can't care.

She says, "His skin. I need his skin."

That stops me. I look at the strange color of her eyes, dark blue-green around the pupil, shading outward to paler green-yellow. When she sees that she has my attention, she explains. "The tanner said he would help me . . . bind our book. We've got just the one. It belonged to our mama."

Dozens of men need my attention urgently. Why do I allow this interruption? Surprise, perhaps. A momentary distraction, possibly necessary. Confrontation with a new kind of urgency. A fleeting reminder of my fiancée, Alice, whom I haven't seen in over a year. Those strange eyes.

I remember seeing Leidy's own copy of his *Elementary Treatise on Human Anatomy*. Inscribed on the flyleaf: "This book is bound in the skin of a Union soldier who died putting down the southern rebellion. The skin was tanned by my own hand in a chamber pot. Joseph Leidy,

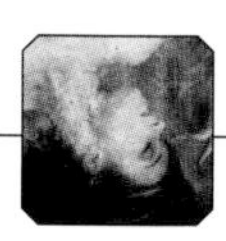

M.D." A gesture of respect. That soldier had been his patient at Satterlee Hospital during the second year of the war.

Anthropodermic bibliopegy—binding books in human skin. An old practice among doctors, who preserve the skins of honored patients *in memoriam*. Human skin is almost impervious to moisture, much more so than other leathers. More supple, easier to work with. And finer, no visible pores.

But it's a difficult craft. Most parts of the human body are too small to yield sufficient leather for the purpose. Thighs, back, and belly—these are the only serviceable parts. Sometimes there's just enough for the spine of the book, so the rest must be bound in another kind of leather.

As for her brother, there's almost nothing left. Wounded, he had lain on his back while the brushfire raged. The unprotected skin of his face and left hand is reddish-black, brittle and flaking. His right hand is just bones. Everywhere else the cotton and wool of his uniform have burned together with his skin and flesh to become an indistinguishable mass.

With its water-load mostly gone, the corpse weighs little. The girl and I lift it onto the table, face down, so I can save what's left: a piece of skin from the upper back, only a few inches square. I wrap the memento in a cloth and hand it to her, saying, "I'm sorry. There's no more." She nods her thanks, then looks at me. Rips a pocket off her apron, reaches up with it to wipe my eyes, my face. Wipes off the blood and sweat. The hysterical tears that ran down my face and dried there, hours ago, when I could still feel.

Then she leans over her brother, kisses the back of his burned head, and leaves. My steward Butler stares after her, then takes her brother's corpse off the table and out the back to the dead wagon. A couple of other stewards swing the next chloroformed and morphined man onto the blood-slippery table. Shattered kneecap, exploded tendons, profuse bleeding. Scalpel and bone saw. I begin cutting again, thinking about the girl and her brother.

The hair of a loved one is a more conventional *memento mori* than the skin—hair clasped in lockets, encased in crystal and gold jewelry,

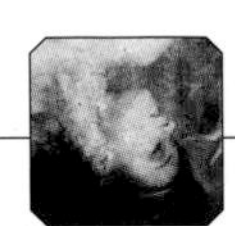

worked into wreaths, embroidered into framed scenes of willows weeping over a grave. Why is saving hair more acceptable than saving skin? Perhaps because the hair cannot be touched once it's under glass. It becomes a work of art, no longer human. Life and death are safely separated.

But a book bound in human skin? Touching it is involuntary. No separation.

Spotsylvania Court House, May 21.

As I enter the dispensary tent, she is leaving. Except for that one glance at her face a couple of weeks ago when she wiped mine, I would never have recognized her: She looks like an infantry soldier. "You?" I say. "What are you doing here?"

She salutes and stands at attention. "Needed calomel, sir. Bloody flux." Holds up a bottle.

I stare. Shaved head. Strange blue-green eyes. Uniform ill-fitting but clean. But her brother's uniform was burned. "Where did you get that uniform?"

"It's mine, sir."

Her brother could have had a second uniform. Or else she stripped a dead comrade. I don't want to know.

I ask, "Who has dysentery?"

"Privates Crozier and Green, sir. And maybe others. Latrine squadron."

"They sent you? What's happening with the latrines?"

"I'll finish the digging when I return, sir. That's why we'll whip them butternuts yet, sir. Shovelry beats chivalry any day."

I look at her. Tall, lean. Brought her brother's body to surgery by herself. Strong. "So you can dig. Can you shoot?"

She looks surprised. "Yes, sir. Raised on a farm. Shot a squirrel at fifty paces when I was seven year old."

After a long moment, I say, "Well, better get back to it, soldier." She salutes and goes.

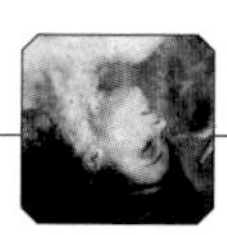

By now we've all heard about the women soldiers who pass for men. Both armies have them. At the beginning of the war, we assumed it was just a few odd ones, but over the years the stories accumulated, as did the respect. Now we know that it's many more than just a few—some say hundreds. And we also know that they're good soldiers. They have to be.

Why don't I turn her in? It's not that I want her. She doesn't provoke lust in me. I barely remember that feeling. Some of the other officers have said the same thing. We think it's the smell. We pretend we're inured to it—sufficiently so that we can perform our duties, at least. But it's always with us.

Open latrines reeking of the feces of thousands of men. And those thousands of men unwashed and stinking in the summer heat. The dung of horses, cattle, pigs, chickens, mules, and dogs. The vomit and diarrhea of the hundreds of men with dysentery. The putrefying flesh of those with gangrene. The ubiquitous vinegar used to wash everything down. Rotting corpses waiting to be buried. And the stale blood everywhere, pungent and fetid.

I remember that my Alice used to wear violet water. Does she still? I try to conjure her scent. Can't.

I take my laundry over to Suds Row. It's against regulations for enlisted men to hang around there when they drop off or pick up, but officers sometimes stop for a brief chat. I stop. Sure enough, I see only three women. "Good morning, ladies. Is one of your number missing in action?"

Number one is boiling, number two is scrubbing, and number three is mending. Numbers one and two look at each other and smile. Number three stands up and walks over to me, saying, "That's right, Captain. Moira done disappeared."

"Moira?"

"Nice Scotch girl. Nova Scotia people. They was living in upstate Pennsylvania when the influenza hit in the fifties. Whole family gone except her and her brother. She come with him when he enlisted. We figure she didn't want to stick around after he was killed."

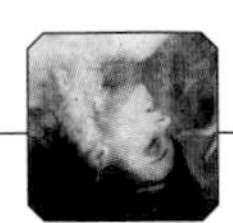

Number one or two calls, "Or else she run off with a soldier." They laugh.

Three says, "Nah, she wouldn't do that. She's a good girl. Real hard worker. This all your laundry for now, Captain?"

"Yes. Thank you. I'll see you next week."

Moira. I'm the only one who knows she didn't run off with a soldier. Or leave because her brother died.

Why not?

I think about those women who mend, wash, dry, and press my uniforms every week. Who are they? Who made and transported those uniforms? Who dyed the cloth, spun and wove the fibers, herded the sheep for the wool, and grew the cotton? Were they men or women? Black or white? Slave or free?

I know nothing about these people, not even their names. But their traces are part of my life.

North Anna River, May 23.

Fitzpatrick's down with the flux, so I'm missing a steward. I send an order to her company commander requesting her transfer to the Invalid Corps for a week so she can assist me in surgery.

She's not as strong as Fitzpatrick, but she's quicker and smarter. She sets up cold water tubs so we can toss in the bloody rags as soon as we're done with them. Says that soaking them in cold water before boiling them will get the blood out better. I hadn't known that.

She's watching me sew a flap of skin over a stump. My only curved suturing needle is long gone, stolen or lost or misplaced, so I'm trying to sew with a straight needle. After a minute, she says, "That works badly, doesn't it?" Takes out her needle case and hands me a curved one. Says it's an upholstery needle. "A surgeon needs it more than a soldier."

When it gets too dark to work and the wounded men are settled in for the night, we make our supper and talk a bit. I ask what happened

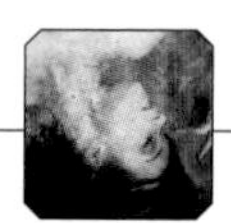

with her brother's skin. She says the tanner saved what he could, but it's too small to bind her book. Shows me the book: an inexpensive edition of Poe's poetry, octavo size, pages stitched together but no binding.

The mellifluous Poe. I was expecting a family Bible or an almanac or a cookbook. Amazed, I ask, "Do you really like this poetry, or do you keep the book only because it belonged to your mother?"

She half closes those strange eyes and says, "I love the poems. I don't know what some of the words mean, but they put me in mind of the sea."

I say, "Murmuring. Susurrating." She smiles at the sounds.

The small square of her brother's tanned skin is stuck into the pages like a bookmark. She hands it to me and says, "Would you write his name on it in ink? Private Benjamin White Gould." Thinks a minute and adds, "Died in the service of his country."

"Yes. I'll do it tonight. Or perhaps you'd like to write it yourself? I can give you pen and ink."

"No, sir. I thank you, but my hand don't write well. I'd like for you to do it."

I nod and take the memento from her. She says, "Mama used to read to us in the evenings. I'd dearly love to hear some of those words again. Would you read out loud?"

In the firelight, my voice startles me. It hasn't pronounced words like this for years.

From childhood's hour I have not been
As others were—I have not seen
As others saw—I could not bring
My passions from a common spring—

As I read, I feel my chest aching. The men's wounds don't hurt me. I don't let them. But these words rake my insides. Childhood's hour. My mother died giving birth to me; my father two years later. I was their only child. Boarding schools were my home, now the army.

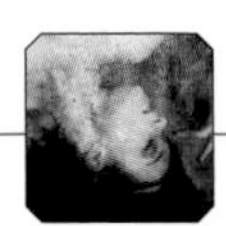

When I finish reading, I look up from the book to see her sitting on the ground, bent knees under her chin, arms around her legs, eyes closed, tears streaking her face. I close my eyes as well, and we sit silently for a few minutes.

After she leaves and I'm writing her brother's name on his skin, I try to remember a time before I could read and write. Can't. I am crammed with education.

I worry that she'll be discovered.

Bethesda Church, May 28.

I'm trying to close a stump that won't stop oozing. There's not enough undamaged skin for me to make a flap. We've run out of styptic. She goes and lights a candle at the fire under the boiling kettle and brings it over to drip hot wax onto the stump. Neatest stump closure I ever saw.

Later, after supper, she silently hands me her book.

O God! can I not grasp
Them with a tighter clasp?
O God! can I not save
One from the pitiless wave?
Is all that we see or seem
But a dream within a dream?

When I read to her this time, I'm expecting the pain, so it doesn't surprise me. I welcome it. And when she weeps, I put my hand on her arm and ask if I can borrow her book for a few nights. I'd like to read some on my own.

Yes.

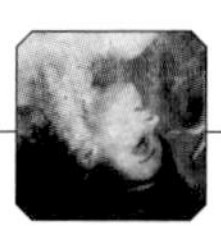

Matadequin Creek, May 30.

She helps the amputees into the ambulance wagon to make the long trip over the corrugated road to the hospital in Washington. I watch her situate each man so his stump is vertical, padding it all around to protect it from jostling, bracing each head with blankets. She winks at a private: "Blakey, you lucky dog! What I wouldn't give for your honorable discharge and pension and comfy carriage ride back home!" Blakey smiles for the first time since I cut off his legs last week. She makes sure the men have water and tobacco. Makes them laugh by saying that the weevils in their hardtack will put them over their meat ration. I watch to see if any of them seem suspicious of her, but there's no sign of it. They don't care about men and women anymore. They're just grateful.

Later I find her inspecting a case of gangrene. The man lay on the ground for two days and a night before he was brought in. When I ask why she isn't cleaning the wound, she says, "Looky here, sir. They're cleaning it." I bend closer and see that she's right: Maggots are eating the black necrotic tissue, leaving healthy pink flesh behind. We leave the man to the maggots, and his fever is down the next day.

I read to her after dark.

See!—it flickers up the sky through the night!
Ah, we safely may trust to its gleaming,
And be sure it will lead us aright—
We safely may trust to a gleaming,
That cannot but guide us aright,
Since it flickers up to Heaven through the night.

The reading pain feels less sharp, more complex tonight. She looks up at the black sky as she listens.

Then she asks if I will keep her book until she comes for it. Her Invalid Corps order has expired, and she will return to battle tomorrow.

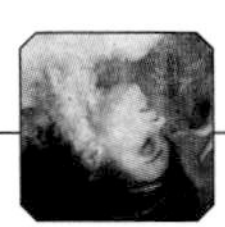

Cold Harbor, June 12.

Nearly two weeks of trench warfare. Unimaginable numbers of dead and wounded, not individuals, just part of the great blood-ocean that covers the earth.

Some of the men bring me bones: skulls, tibias, femurs. They find them on the battlefield. Not from full-fleshed corpses, not from the current battle. Bare bones—cleaned by maggots, rats, and vultures—from our comrades who died in this same place two years back.

I sometimes snatch a few minutes to read from her book.

And we passed to the end of the vista,
But were stopped by the door of a tomb—
By the door of a legended tomb;
And I said: "What is written, sweet sister,
On the door of this legended tomb?"
She replied: "Ulalume—Ulalume—
'Tis the vault of thy lost Ulalume!"

I no longer notice any pain when I read. Maybe it's been absorbed into something else.

One of the men from the 4th Delaware brings her in. He remembers her assisting me in surgery that week. Upper chest and shoulder wound, bled to death in twenty minutes or so. Exsanguination. She would have smiled at the sound of that lovely word. The death of Private Benjamin White Gould—her brother—is already recorded in the register, so I make no official notation of her death. I take her body out and hide it in my tent.

We're in enemy territory. We bury our dead hastily, in shallow graves, in fields of sweet potatoes and cotton and tobacco. When the Rebs find the graves, the bodies are unearthed and stripped, left to bloat under the sun. Left for crows and vultures—sometimes, we've heard, fed

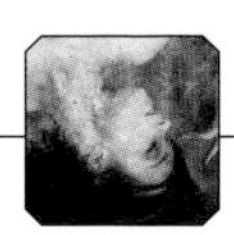

to the hogs. But even if the Rebs don't find the bodies, others will: raccoons and opossums, weasels and bobcats. Coyotes.

She deserves better.

I remember the tanner's advice: thighs, back, belly.

With a dull knife, I scrape the bits of fat and muscle from inside the skin, slowly detaching the clinging veins. A husband would have taken pleasure in touching this skin. But now it must be a reader.

I empty some of the urine from the bladder into a porcelain bowl, adding lime and wood ash. Working slowly, I apply the mixture to the outside of the greening skin. If she had ever given birth, would the child have looked like her? With the same red-gold hair? These fine, almost invisible hairs that I now scrape away as gently as I can.

The dark blue-green eyes are filmed over with a cloudy pale gray. Rigor mortis has already receded, so I can close the lids. Flatten the curved fingers. Cover her hand with mine.

Opening the skull, I remove the brain and heat it over a low fire. When it begins to bubble, I take it off the flame. Stir it with salt and the remainder of the urine. Working slowly, I apply the mixture to both sides of the skin. I think about my fiancée, of the intimacy of married life. What would it be like? Like having another self? Being one person in two bodies? I hope I will know someday.

Cutting open the colon, I remove and dilute the feces. Smooth the watery dung over the skin, watching it relax and lie flat. I always called her Private Gould. I never said her real name.

After rinsing the skin, I stretch it on a board and drive nails around the outside to keep it flat, to prevent it from shrinking as it dries. I run the tips of my fingers lightly over it.

Moira.

BLACK BODIES

Rural South Carolina, 1901

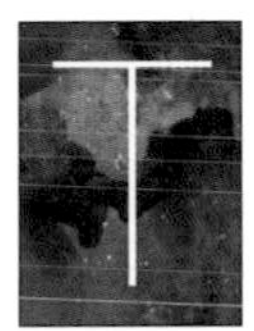

he doctor watched as his two assistants took Anthea's clothes before helping her up onto the table. Six months into her fifth pregnancy, she was a bit clumsy. The men slid their forearms under her elbows and lifted her to sit on the edge.

Jerome bent to make a stirrup of his hands for Anthea's feet to push against. He'd done this same thing for her that time in the Murphys' barn. She'd run in when he'd been mucking out stalls and begged him to hide her. Said Dusty had taken after her again. She'd been just a slip of a girl then. Jerome had boosted her over the door of a stall, and the quiet old mare in there never blinked. When Dusty charged in, Jerome had said, "Yes, I seen her a while ago, but I don't see her now." He didn't like to lie. After Dusty stormed away, Jerome had opened the stall door to let Anthea out. Her eyes had been real big and white.

Lucian held Anthea's armpits to help her move back onto the table. That she should need his help frightened him. When he was just a baby with pneumonia, Anthea had helped his mother nurse him back to the world. He didn't remember being sick, of course, but his mother gloried in telling him how he wouldn't be around today if Aunt Anthea hadn't been there. Anthea had even postponed her own wedding until she was sure young Lucian was well enough to do without her. All these years

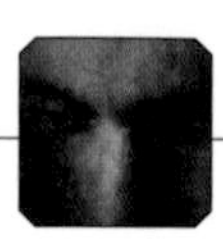

later, Uncle Henry still joked that he could have gotten a head start in his marriage bed if it hadn't been for Lucian.

Anthea finally sat, legs at full length, and the three men waited a moment while she tried to catch her breath. This baby seemed lighter than she remembered the others being. Still plenty heavy to carry around, though.

When Anthea's breathing slowed, Jerome and Lucian helped her turn over into cow position, resting on her hands and knees, swollen breasts dangling, nipples erect in response to the cold January morning. Her head moved up and down, finding no rest.

The doctor saw that the patient needed a more comfortable position. Depending on what he discovered presently, the work ahead might take as much as an hour. He shook his head, irritated at himself for not thinking more clearly. But, after all, he was the first medical man to work seriously on this problem. Everything was an experiment. "No, that won't work. Sims position, please."

Jerome stepped forward to help Anthea lie on her left front, moving her left arm under her head. Must have been pretty soon after that time in the barn that Mama had died, and Anthea's folks had taken him in. He'd been fifteen or so—could have made it on his own—but it had been real Christian of them. And he could keep a better eye on young Anthea, keep her out of Dusty's reach. No point in worrying her folks about it.

Lucian moved Anthea's left knee to meet the right, her feet spread apart. In the beginning of the doctor's time, when Lucian had tried to apologize for having to touch her in this way, for having to see her naked, she had looked down and shaken her head. "You ain't done nothing wrong. No need to apologize. No need to talk about it." Her voice had been just a whisper. He never corrected her grammar or pronunciation, but she knew she didn't speak well. Whenever she found him helping Phebe and Nick with their lessons, she always squeezed his shoulder in thanks.

The vagina now open, Lucian held the reflecting lantern to illuminate inside as much as possible. Jerome readied the fine silver wire for suturing. The doctor picked up his speculum.

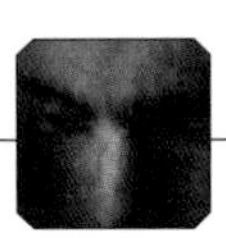

The doctor's life was devoted to helping the weaker sex, condemned by their pathological anatomies to derangement of the moral sense and infantilization of the intellect. Whenever he lost a patient in childbirth, he felt the failure as personal, as though he himself were the bereaved husband and father. On those days, he sequestered himself in his study, rereading the medical texts that might have helped him and praying for God's forgiveness of his inadequacies as a physician. When his grateful patients and their families thanked him through sobs for his services or kissed his hand in gratitude, he modestly redirected their gratitude to God.

Rarely did he venture outside his small sphere. He had attended a regional gynecological conference at the medical college in Charleston a few years back, but the experience had been so unpleasant that he had returned home early to avoid conversing with his presumptuous and callow colleagues. Such men! So wild and speculative in their theories, so radical in their procedures—removing cervixes to relieve sterility, removing uteruses to relieve hysteria, removing clitorises to relieve masturbation. He would have enjoyed a collegial relationship with another empirically minded physician, but God had assigned him to work alone.

And so he had cast his lot with his rural patients. At least they had him. Many colored people had no medical man at all and had to make do with unschooled midwives and herbalists. He sighed. Hoodoo women, root doctors, conjure workers. And, though he had no intellectual colleagues, Jerome and Lucian were excellent assistants. They were invaluable not only because of their obedience and strength, but also because of their understanding of his patients. When a patient could not articulate her symptoms understandably, through either fear or lack of an educated vocabulary, Jerome and Lucian could sometimes interpret for him. He hated starting an examination with no idea of the problem. It wasted time and made him look foolish.

This morning there would be no such impediment. Anthea had been his patient for ten years, and he already knew the problem: a vesicovaginal fistula. Though not life-threatening or painful, this condition was

highly unpleasant, causing distress to the sufferer and to those around her. The constant involuntary discharge of urine through the vagina rendered Anthea useless for indoor service, so she had been assigned farmyard duties. It also made her unpleasant for Henry to impregnate, so her offspring had not been as frequent as they should have been. Vesicovaginal fistula was a common enough problem that one would have thought its correction would also be common, but such was not the case. The historical record showed very few successful surgical corrections.

The doctor was very close to a solution, having experimented for more than ten years with this patient and her similarly afflicted sisters. He had entirely discredited the popular but ineffective technique of coagulation by the application of silver nitrate. He had improved upon his first speculum—a bent pewter spoon—and now had instruments of his own design manufactured from surgical-grade steel. Having discarded Mettauer's recommendation of using silk or gut sutures to repair the fistula, the doctor now used fine silver wire custom-made by a Charleston jeweler, costly but permanent and antiseptic. He had documented and published his preliminary findings in *The American Journal of the Medical Sciences*, emphasizing the need for accurate resection of the vagina and postoperative bladder catheterization. And he had done all this without payment from his patients. Everything had been accomplished with his own funds and those of his patients' employers.

Today—victory! Thanks be to God! This examination revealed the culmination of his years of work: a week after his thirtieth surgery on this patient, there was no inflammation, no tumefaction, and a perfect repair of the fistula.

He withdrew the speculum and set it on the table. Lucian would sterilize and store it later. He smiled at his assistants, said, "We've won, boys!" and stepped to the basin to wash his hands. "Jerome, tell the patients waiting outside to return tomorrow." He'd take the rest of the day off to enjoy a leisurely victory meal at home and to work on his final report for publication.

As the doctor left the room, Lucian and Jerome exchanged glances. Jerome turned to retrieve Anthea's clothes from the nail he had hung them on. She had sewn this skirt a long time back. This blue cloth was part of the load that he and Henry had brought back from Charleston that time. Must have been before the doctor come, because there had been no one living in the big house to ask about taking the wagon, so they just took it. Henry had wanted to get her the red, but Jerome knew she'd like the blue better. Still wearing that same old skirt.

Meanwhile, Lucian covered Anthea with the ancient wool quilt he took from the back of the clinic's only chair. His grandmother's quilt. She'd been rescued from bondage when the Union fleet liberated Saint Catherine's Island in 1862. Captain Whitmore had taken a shine to her because she could read and write. Even though she was only fourteen, the captain had asked her to organize and run a school for all the colored children freed from that island. That had been the beginning of her lifelong teaching career, and all his family had been book people ever since. His mother treasured the quilt, of course, but when she learned that there was no covering for the doctor's patients, she'd told Lucian to put it in the clinic. The doctor had never said anything about it, so it must be all right.

Anthea shivered when the scratchy wool touched her skin. The table was still cold underneath her. Inhaling deeply, she pushed herself back up into cow position, feeling Lucian hold the quilt to cover her back and shoulders, waiting to turn over until Jerome had laid her clothes nearby. Those two were more ashamed than she was. She'd done this so many times she didn't feel naked no more, just cold. Would be nice to be able to set her bare feet on a rug when she got down off the table. Then she pursed her lips. Aw, shoo, woman. Cold feet is nothing. Be glad you got feet that still walk.

When she finally stood on the chilly boards, huddling the quilt around her, she nodded her thanks to Lucian and Jerome. They turned discreetly aside to perform other tasks while she dressed herself.

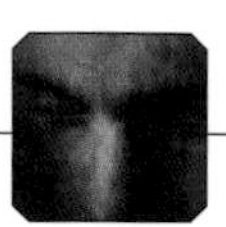

As he ate, the doctor sifted through the morning's mail: an advertising circular from a medical supply company, an announcement of a forthcoming conference, a letter from his daughter away at the Salem Female Academy, the jeweler's bill for the latest batch of silver wire. But what was this Chicago postmark? He opened and scanned the typed letter in silence as Meme, his serving maid, looked out the frosty window.

> **Dear Sir:**
>
> **I am the science and medicine correspondent for several major newspapers and magazines, including *The New York Times*, *The Washington Post*, and *Harper's*. A mutual acquaintance of ours, Dr. Silas Weir Mitchell, whom I met through his literary contributions to *The Atlantic Monthly*, kindly informed me of your important work in the repair of the vesicovaginal fistula. He suggested that an interview with you might serve as the basis for an article that would be read with much interest by many physicians and women along the East Coast.**
>
> **I shall be in Charleston next month on business. Before I return to Chicago, and if agreeable to you, I should like to interview you. I could be in Ravenel on the afternoon of February 22. The interview would require approximately one hour. If possible, I would also like to see and photograph the medical facility which you have so generously created to serve the impoverished women of your area.**
>
> **I would appreciate receiving your response before February 15, the day I depart on my travels.**
>
> **Yours very sincerely,**
> ***I. M. Clavell***

The signature was large, strong, and plain, the hand of confidence. That every paragraph began with "I" certainly attested to the man's healthy ego. But why not? Correspondent for several of the nation's

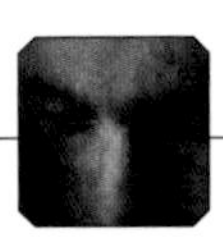

leading newspapers and magazines? The doctor had never dreamed of publicizing his work to such a large population. A few articles in scholarly journals had been his modest goal. And that Weir Mitchell, the famous neurologist, had remembered and recommended his work to this journalist was wonderfully flattering. An article in *The Atlantic Monthly* could be his entrée into a world of larger possibilities. God was good.

Holding Clavell's letter and envelope, the doctor hurried from the table. Meme picked up the other mail, left unopened next to his dirty plate. What was Lucian waiting for? She had made it plain as day that she wanted him, going out of her way to walk across the yard where he was working, walking real slow, her hips dancing up and down to make him watch her. He wouldn't look if he didn't want her, so why the wait? Sister Annie was already married, and she a year younger than Meme. Time's a-wasting. She straightened the doctor's letters into a neat pile and set them on the sideboard.

The doctor normally accepted gratitude from his patients and their families in products such as fresh eggs and vegetables or in domestic services such as gardening and housecleaning. But now he added clinic renovation to the list. He explained the situation to his patients' employers, all of whom were willing for their servants to help out as long as their regular work didn't suffer. So he sent word by way of old Ben, his usual boy, to his patients and their families that medical treatments would cease until after the journalist's visit. Instead, the time allotted for them to help him would be spent on sprucing up the clinic.

The work proceeded fairly well—always slower than he wanted, of course, but that was the nature of the labor force. And he did have to keep an eye on the workers to make sure that jobs were done to his standards. Fortunately, the weather cooperated. The clinic building (a converted chicken coop) got its first coats of white paint inside and out,

as did his desk, the examination table, and the storage cabinet (all the furniture donations in lieu of payment). Now it looked like the *sanctum sanctorum* it truly was: clean and bright. It would photograph well. He watched Lucian laying flat stones to serve as a walkway across the muddy yard. If there was time after that work was finished, he'd ask the boy to dig in some early spring bulbs along the path. With God's grace, they might bloom in time for the journalist's visit.

Lucian worked steadily. Slow down, boy. Don't break your back on this job. You don't want to end up like Jerome, stiff and bent before his time, older than his forty-odd years. Works like a draft horse. Trying to keep himself busy so as not to moon over Nora running off with that half-breed. Flighty bitch.

Meanwhile, Jerome sawed a couple of square holes in the walls of the chicken coop. How does the doctor see anything at all when he looks into Anthea's private place? So dark in there, so dark in this room. And the nasty smell after the surgeries, when she's been bleeding. The windows'll let in air and light but also cold. If Lucian would hustle with laying them stones, he could help finish up with this sawing.

The doctor was expecting Anthea to bring the new window curtains, but it was a young girl who picked her way across the new stepping-stones with the fresh white cotton draped over her outstretched arms. He met her at the clinic door to relieve her burden and carefully laid the curtains over the back of the chair, on top of the smelly old quilt that someone had put there. He'd have to toss that thing out before the journalist arrived. "Ah, at last! The finishing touch. Thank you very much. Where is Anthea?" The girl murmured something, her face downcast. "Speak up, young missy. I can't hear you."

The girl raised her head a bit but still did not meet his eyes. "Home with the baby."

But Anthea wasn't due for two months yet! Startled, the doctor began to ask why he hadn't been called, but then he remembered that old

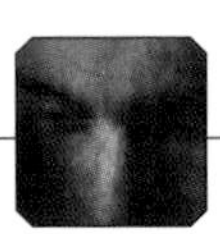

Ben had put out the word that medical services had been suspended for a few weeks. "When did she have the baby?"

"'St'day." The sound registered belatedly as "yesterday."

"Who helped her?"

"Dr. Lewis."

His mouth drew down. No "doctor" about old Tilly, the midwife. Probably pulled the baby out by its head. He'd be amazed if any premature infant delivered by her managed to survive. "Ah. Well, thank you again. You may go." He turned away, and the small girl began to pick her way back across the slippery rocks.

Lucian looked up from the stone he was setting in place and said, "Mind how you go, honey." Jerome had told him that Anthea had looked just like that when she was ten years old.

Inside the clinic, Jerome was already stringing the white curtains on wires that he had nailed across the windows. That new baby weak. Henry ought to see about getting the christening done directly. Sunday might be too late. All that mucking about inside her must of made it come too early. Sometimes all the schooling in the world don't make a man wise.

After automatically checking to make sure the wire Jerome was using was plain lead, not the expensive custom-made silver, the doctor asked, "Did you see that girl just now? The one with the red rag on her head? Who was that?"

Without turning from his task, Jerome said, "Anthea's girl. Phebe."

The doctor said irritably, "No, no! That child died."

"This the second Phebe. The first one born and died the year the canker killed the red oaks." That baby never breathed right, not from the start. Anthea watched and prayed—everyone did—as that poor infant had tried and tried to breathe. Hurt to watch her. A blessing when she died.

"Oh, right. Before my time. You people. Two daughters with the same name. How am I supposed to keep all these babies straight?"

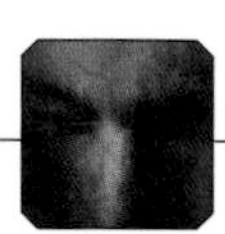

Jerome carefully spread the gathers of the curtain across the wire. "Phebe, sir. After Anthea's mama. This Phebe the one you delivered."

"Ah, now I remember. Yes, a good girl. Strong and healthy. I don't remember ever having to treat her."

"Last year, sir. She had that infection." Anthea had been wild with worry. Two babies already dead and this second Phebe burning up with fever. When the girl got better, Anthea had said, "It don't matter what he do to me. He saved her."

"Right, right. You've got a fine memory, Jerome, much better than mine. It's a good thing you're around to help me out."

Jerome stood back to inspect the curtains. "Yes, sir."

All was in order by the afternoon of February 22. The doctor sat on his back porch, reading and smoking. The blacks stayed out of sight but alert for service inside their mud-chinked wooden cabins.

Jerome straddled his stool, hammering nails into the new leather sole he was attaching to one of the doctor's boots. Nora had been gone for over six months now, and the smell of her body was lost to him forever, but he still heard her voice. Just snippets, bits and pieces, but pretty much all the time. Right after she left, he tried not to hear, tried to cover up that voice with his own singing or talking or praying. Now, though, he was easier with its company: the laughter that ran up into his brain like a squirrel scrambling up a tree, the soft humming while she combed and smoothed her glossy hair, the names she had called him to get his goat—*uncle* and *old man* (even though she was older by a couple of years), *J'room* (to make light of his saint's name), and, when he fussed at her carelessness, *mammy*. Jerome sighed, looked out his window at the cold white sky, and picked up the doctor's other boot.

The doctor knew that the journalist would arrive by carriage, not riverboat, so his first view would be of the ramshackle rear of the house

rather than the better-tended front. Not that the house wasn't significant—it had been built just before the war as a summer home for an important family of plantation owners, giving them an escape from the humidity, disease, and insects of the hot season. In winter, as now, the timber-framed house was naturally cold, but it was still an interesting example of the Carolina farmhouse style from the West Indies. It had been quite a while since the doctor had had the opportunity to explain the history of the place to a visitor. He had dug up his old local history notes so he could refresh his memory while he waited.

He settled into his rocking chair, where he'd be able to see the carriage before it arrived. The angel oaks, once a well-trimmed *allée,* had spread their wings so wide across the dirt road that they blocked the sunlight and brushed the higher-riding carriage drivers' caps with fronds of dripping Spanish moss. He'd have plenty of time to damp his pipe, set aside his notes, stand, and straighten his attire before the journalist alighted.

While the doctor was reading outdoors, Lucian was reading indoors. Availing himself of the doctor's classical library, he was looking into the works of that other Lucian, the ancient satirist of Samosata. Painstakingly comparing the snippets of English translation in Hime's biography with the original texts in the Dindorf edition, he was teaching himself Latin and (much less successfully) Lucian's Attic Greek dialect. But the attraction was not so much a love of the words, of their sounds and shapes, as of the astonishing new ideas they represented. "The most necessary quality for success is ignorance, coupled with impudence, boldness, and effrontery. Leave modesty, equity, and blushes at home." Lucian's mouth twisted. Modesty? That was Jerome's affliction, not his. Equity? He had a harder time with that one, still laboring under the illusion that it was a good thing. Blushes? Hell, the doctor hadn't even recognized Phebe! He wouldn't notice a black man blushing at point-blank range.

The doctor's reading was interrupted by a distant growl and a repeated, aggressive hooting. Startled, he pocketed his notes and pipe, then stood and stepped back until his shoulders felt the comfort of the

house wall. From the far end of the long dirt road a whirling cloud of dust hurtled incomprehensively toward him.

By the time his mind processed the phenomenon, the carriage had stopped thirty feet away. Horseless. He had seen a few motorcars in Charleston, of course. From a distance. But he had certainly never seen one in Ravenel. As the driver pulled off his tight cap and goggles and swung his legs out the open side, the doctor nervously looked around. Eyes peeked from the cabin windows, but he felt quite alone as he waited to greet his guest.

"Hello, Dr. Mangan. I'm Ida Clavell." A female. God preserve us. She had slipped off her gauntlets and was extending her right hand. He blinked, ducked his head, and met the hand with his own. Hers jammed itself against his, squeezed his fingers, and pumped up and down three times before releasing. He couldn't yet look at her; his eyes had automatically turned to the motorcar. The female said, "A wonderful monster, eh? Edith Wharton says that motoring offers 'an immense enlargement of life,' and I agree. When I had my first ride a few years ago, I promised myself that I'd buy a car as soon as I could. This one is a Stevens-Duryea runabout."

He had never ridden in a motorcar. He didn't know who Edith Wharton was. "But aren't they very expensive?"

The journalist laughed as she beat the dust out of her long coat. "Oh, yes. I would have paid over a thousand dollars for this one if I'd bought it new, but I acquired it for half-price from my boss after he bought a faster one. Black Bess here has only a two-cylinder, five-horsepower engine, so she goes no more than forty miles an hour. His new automobile goes over sixty."

A thousand dollars, more than his entire last year's income. Sixty miles an hour, twice as fast as a galloping horse. Dear God—why? The doctor shook his head. "You . . . you drove that car from Chicago? But that's . . . that's hundreds of miles."

"Yep. Over nine hundred. It's a contest. My sister recently drove from Detroit to New York City, more than six hundred miles. I wanted to best her."

Incredible. Now that he could look at her face, he saw that she was at least forty, a bit horse-faced, plainly dressed. He glanced at her left hand: no ring, no surprise. Had probably taken up this dangerous sport as a compensation for spinsterhood.

"Very interesting. And how long did this road trip take you, Miss Clavell?"

"It's Mrs." She held up her naked left hand. "I don't wear my ring under my driving gloves. My husband is also a journalist. He doesn't drive my car, and I don't drive his." She laughed. "It took me less than four days to drive here. Would have taken twice that long on the train."

"And how does your husband feel about your solo expedition into the wilds of South Carolina?" The doctor was beginning to recover his wits.

"He said, 'Send me a postcard,' so I bought these in Charleston." The doctor automatically took the cards she handed him.

The first card showed a photograph of three watermelon-eating pickaninnies, hand-colored so their skin was an unnaturally even dark brown, like shoe polish, that contrasted brilliantly with their painted white teeth. The verse printed over the photograph read: "Shoo, you melancholy, though we has not a dime, / Us niggers has no worries in watermelon time."

The doctor chuckled. He'd seen similar cards many times, but they always tickled him.

The journalist was looking at him, not at the card. She said, "Amusing? Here, take it. I have others." He accepted the card, still smiling, and pocketed it.

The second card showed a photograph of two adolescent black boys hanging from a telegraph pole. The barefoot boys hung chest to chest, the taller one's chin resting on top of the other one's head. A few of the white faces in the crowd below smiled at the camera; a few white hands waved. Just another version of the many lynching cards popular among the rabble. Probably a novelty to a Northerner.

Meanwhile, in the big house, Meme went through the doctor's dirty

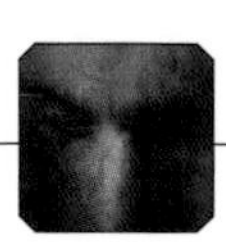

laundry, sorting out the things that Anthea needed to mend before they were washed. That man was right careless with his linen—these black spots spattered on his cuffs wouldn't wash out come hell or high water. It'd probably be just the same with Lucian. Both just as uppity as could be; neither one know how to treat a woman. Well, the doctor she couldn't do nothing about. But Lucian—once she got him into her bed, she'd teach him something about respect.

After glancing at the photograph of the two hanging black boys, the doctor told the journalist, "I wouldn't have thought this photograph to your taste."

She replied sharply, "It's the activity that's not to my taste. The photograph is merely a historical document." She took the cards from his hand (even though he hadn't seen them all) and returned them to her bag.

He nodded, confused by her sudden coolness. His social invitation—"Would you care to take some refreshment in the house before seeing the clinic?"—sounded less enthusiastic than he intended, so he was not surprised when she refused.

He led the way. Once they were inside the bright white room, he talked while she took notes and photographs. He told her about his medical education, his desire to improve women's medical care after his young wife had died of peritonitis following the birth of his daughter. About his decision (at God's direction) to forgo the immediate rewards of an urban medical practice in order to take the time necessary to conduct careful experiments that might lead to real improvements in surgical practice. About his decision to put his welfare second to that of his patients by maintaining a medical practice for poor blacks at his own expense. About his recent victory over that long-standing enemy of women, the vesico-vaginal fistula.

Meanwhile, inside the cabin assigned to Henry's family, Phebe stood with her back to the barely warm coal stove, watching her mother nurse the fussy baby, watching her wince when he sucked her sore, cracked nipple. The girl silently retrieved the comfrey salve from the washstand

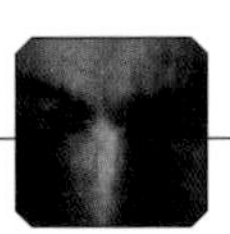

and held it out to her mother. Anthea smiled and whispered her thanks, said, "I'll put some on just as soon as he gets done." Phebe continued to watch the ugly pinkish-brown face with its hungry mouth suck out her mother's strength. It occurred to her for the first time, but not the last, that she would not have children, ever.

In the clinic, the doctor continued to talk. The journalist was a gratifying listener, nodding in understanding and asking for more details. The doctor had begun to warm up to her when she said, "I see—or rather smell—that this room was recently painted. But of course whiteness isn't the same thing as antisepsis. What are your sterilization procedures?"

He was proud to answer, "I and my assistants wash our hands with hot water and soap before and after each procedure. The speculum and other instruments are submerged in a carbolic acid bath immediately before use. As I hope you know, many other surgeons are much less careful about sterilization."

She was writing and didn't look up when she asked, "And the examination table?"

"Well, it's wiped down with carbolic acid before and after each use, but wood, even painted wood, cannot be truly sterilized."

"And your plans for acquiring a metal table?"

The digression annoyed him. "As I believe I have already mentioned, all the furniture in this clinic has been donated. I would certainly accept a metal table if one were offered."

"Why not buy one? You could raise the funds from your patients' employers. Everyone would benefit from less illness among the patients."

"Yes, that's so. And I trust God will provide. Now, if—"

"You've mentioned your assistants, Lucian and Jerome. Have you no female assistants? To put your patients more at ease?"

His neck stiffened. "My entire life is dedicated to putting my patients more at ease. But as for assistants, males are stronger and more obedient, less prone to illness."

"Ah, yes. The female pathological anatomy. But wouldn't your patients

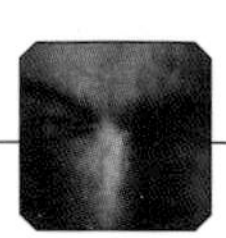

be more likely to talk to other women about their problems? Your research might benefit if they spoke up more."

Why couldn't she stick to the subject? "No, I need quiet to work, not females chattering. And now our time—"

"Just one more question, please. How do you sedate or anesthetize your patients for surgery? Ether, chloroform, opium?"

"No, just a tot of whiskey if the patient seems nervous. She needs to be awake in order for me to record her responses to stimuli, including pain. The experimental nature of the surgery requires it, I'm afraid. Fortunately, the Negress is a hardier breed who feels pain to a lesser degree than her fairer sister." A commonly known fact. God's will.

Now the journalist looked up from her notes, eyebrows lifted. "I'm confused. If women are too weak and prone to illness to serve as medical assistants, how can they simultaneously be so strong that they don't feel pain?"

Irritated, he said, "You are indeed confused, my dear. You may recall that I was speaking specifically of the Negress, whose musculature and constitution can take more punishment than those of the white lady."

"And yet you experiment upon black women in order to improve medical treatment for white women. So their bodies must be the same, at least under the skin. Mustn't they?"

God is our strength. "Mrs. Clavell, the complexities of the racial differences in female anatomy cannot be explained in a few words. Medical men require many years of schooling to understand such concepts." Seeing her open her mouth again, he continued, "I fear we must conclude this interview now. I know you will do the best you can with the information I was able to give you during my limited time today. If you would care to send me a copy of the article before publication, I shall be happy to amend any errors that may have occurred in the drafting." His hand was touching her waist, steering her toward the door.

She twisted away from his touch but continued toward the door. "I'm afraid my publication deadline allows no time for manuscript

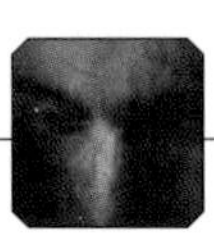

corrections by subject experts. But I will certainly send you a copy of the article after it's published." At the door, she turned toward him and extended her hand, which he again accepted automatically. "Thank you for your time, Dr. Mangan. On behalf of all women, I appreciate the work that you are doing to improve our medical care. I have learned a great deal today." After the squeeze and the three pumps, she released his hand and turned to walk to her car, pulling her goggles, cap, and gauntlets from her bag as she did so. He watched from the doorway as she cranked her engine smartly, vaulted up into her seat through the open side of the car, and drove away, waving farewell with one gauntlet.

He raised one hand to waist level but dropped it before it waved. Muckraker. God forgive her.

Inside Henry's cabin, her back now turned to the baby who probably wouldn't live, Anthea peered through a chink in the mud plaster at the powerful black motorcar disappearing into the distance. *Distance,* a word she'd never needed to pronounce. Distance, a stranger to her. She would never know distance, speed, power, flight. Jerome had told her that the ocean was not very far away, but she had never seen it. And young Lucian—he yearned to go but was afraid because this was the only place he'd ever known.

Now the car was gone. Eyes closed, Anthea turned back toward the restlessly sleeping child. She felt Phebe watching her.

The doctor returned to his sullied clinic. After walking a few paces to and fro, attending to his inhalation and exhalation, he stepped to one of the windows and roughly pulled the new white curtain aside, tearing a bit of Anthea's careful stitching.

Fresh air. Better.

Reaching into his jacket pocket for his pipe, he felt and then removed the amusing postcard that the journalist had given him, and he smiled at it again. After all, God was good. Her article would surely bring favorable attention to his work and income to his practice. He might even buy that metal examination table after all.

HALF-LIFE

Philadelphia, 1921

THE COLLEGE OF PHYSICIANS OF PHILADELPHIA
IS PROUD TO SPONSOR
MADAME MARIE CURIE
WHO WILL PRESENT HER QUARTZ PIEZO ELECTRIQUE APPARATUS
FOR MEASURING THE RADIO-ACTIVITY OF RADIUM
MONDAY EVENING, MAY 23, 1921, AT 8:30 P.M.
ADMISSION EXCLUSIVE TO HOLDERS OF THIS CARD.

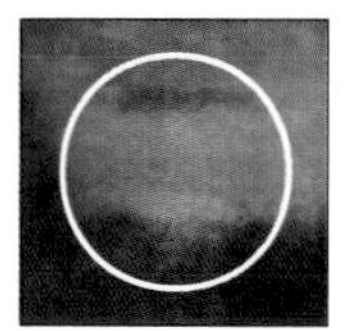

h, how she hated celebrity! All this traveling and eating and smiling and thanking and demurring—so tiresome. Such a waste of precious time. She was no longer young, and there was still so much work to do. Six weeks for this American tour, all the while accumulating heavy wooden plaques, childish gold and silver medals, useless doctoral robes, framed certificates, and other detritus that she'd have to carry in her luggage or pay to have shipped home to Paris. But this was the sacrifice she had to make for the radium, the precious gram she needed to keep the work going. Although Americans were generous with their vast wealth, they certainly claimed their pound of flesh in hand-shaking.

Most of the events required only her brief appearance, not a full-blown lecture. Tonight would be difficult: an audience consisting entirely of ambitious, highly educated men challenged by her celebrity, her prizes, and especially her femaleness. She was tired of proving herself over and over to such people. Their questions demanded ridiculous speculation on her part ("What do you see as the future application of radioactivity to medicine?") or required her to condense thirty years of work into a one-minute response ("How did you reach your conclusion that radium has an individual chemical identity separate from that of polonium?"). The point of such questions was to exhibit the knowledge of the questioner, not to elicit technical information from her. Those who really wanted such information knew where it was published. And if she hesitated or stumbled in her answer, or if she failed to project her voice sufficiently so everyone could hear, she could practically feel the pedestal crumbling underneath her.

She chastised herself: This train of thought was ungrateful and unproductive. She was just exhausted and worried. Her tenuous professional position and the poor research facilities at the Sorbonne had always made the work more difficult than it should have been.

And that stupid scandal had really slowed her down. If she needed to lash out at someone, it should be Paul's horrid wife, Jeanne. That cow! No intellect—a breeder, nothing more. First she kicked Paul out of the house for choosing the altruistic cause of science over a more profitable job that would pay for her fripperies. Next she arranged for Paul's apartment to be broken into and Marie's private letters to him stolen and published in the newspaper. Stupidest of all, Jeanne's brother had challenged Paul to a duel, and, unbelievably, he had accepted. A duel—in the twentieth century! No one had been hurt, so the climax had been a circus, not a tragedy.

She petulantly kicked one foot against the inner ankle of the other while maintaining her smile and eye contact with the well-upholstered gentleman who was regaling her about some earth-shattering topic. She

sometimes thought she might have preferred the tragedy, whatever the outcome.

When the scandal had broken, crowds gathered around Marie's house and threw rocks, smashing windowpanes and terrorizing her daughters. The family had taken refuge in a friend's house for a year. Marie had skulked in the dark, doing no work, accomplishing nothing except the sale of the damaged house—the house where she had lived with Pierre. Not so long ago, she had been hailed as a savior of humanity, a saint, the foremost scientist of the age. How quickly the press and public had reduced her to trollop, homewrecker, whore.

Stop it! she told herself. Those who had harassed her were ignorant and vicious, yes, but also human. The whole point of her work had always been to better the condition of humanity (there being no God to do so), as she had done in setting up the mobile radiology laboratories during the Great War. She had saved the limbs and lives of thousands of soldiers with that service. Her American press contacts had publicized her good work while charitably suppressing the scandal. That was one of the reasons she had said yes to this American tour, out of gratitude.

She needed a few minutes of quiet before making her presentation. Excusing herself from the upholstered gentleman, she ducked out a side door and found herself delightfully alone in a brick-walled garden. Looking around, she recognized many of the plants: feverfew, clary sage, aconite, bee balm, foxglove, lady's mantle—all medicinal herbs. That made sense for a college of physicians. But some of the plants were unfamiliar, perhaps native to North America. That tall bush with the licorice-mint scent and lavender-blue glow? She bent to read the label: *Agastache foeniculum* (anise hyssop). The scent was not sweet but green, sappish—definitely sexual. A few late-day bees penetrated the tubular bells of the flowers.

How she had loved her honeymoon with Pierre, bicycling through the French countryside, exploring the woods and meadows. That had been more than twenty-five years ago, and she still thought of it nearly every day. They had traveled light, buying bread and cheese along the

way, rinsing out their socks in the streams, spreading their blankets on fragrant pine needles. The best part was that no one knew where they were. Days of solitude and leisure.

Paul, always a fantasist, had promised her vacations and pleasure trips if she would marry him. But it wouldn't have been the same thing at all.

Pierre had been the teacher of her youth, her guide as they tramped through the woods to their secret picnic spot inside the old abandoned stone folly. Its windows were so covered with ancient woody vines that no one could have seen them inside—not that there was anyone around for miles. Most of what she knew, Pierre had taught her: French, physics, mathematics, instrumentation, sex. When he had grumbled about her terrible cooking (she was not interested, resentful of time spent away from work), she shot back that he should have taught her to cook if he expected her to do it. Then they both had laughed because he had known no more about cooking than she.

But after Pierre's death, she became the teacher and Paul the student—Paul, a married man with four children. Very different! The Nobel committee had even asked her to stay away from Stockholm to avoid tainting the precious ceremony. She had not really wanted to make the long trip, but after that insult, she made sure to be there. If she had been a man, her prize would never have been jeopardized in that outrageous manner.

She had reminded Paul that if they did marry, the scandal of their illicit liaison would be fueled by fresh outrage over his divorce. She would certainly lose her chair at the Sorbonne, as well as her skimpy research facilities. Paul might even lose his job, and then where would they be, having to support her two children and his four? Not to mention Jeanne, his cow-wife.

A baritone voice startled her: "Have you come out to enjoy the lovely evening?"

Solitude lost again! But her jolt of annoyance was tempered by a pleasant frisson: He had addressed her in French, using the informal

second-person pronoun. She had never really been comfortable with "*vous*" and "Madame" and "Professor"; they made her feel so old and pretentious. And after six weeks of getting by in English (the worst of her five languages), she felt the stranger's *tu* as a kiss on the cheek.

She looked around and saw him leaning casually against the brick wall, smoking. He did not hold his cigarette like an American, between thumb and forefinger, as though pinching an insect to death. He held it between forefinger and middle finger, loosely but assuredly, secure in his command of the thing. Tall, very thin, thirtyish, with reddish-brown hair and fair skin. An astonishing straight line from top of forehead to tip of nose. He looked at her unsmiling but with interested eyes.

What did he see? A graying woman in her fifties, tired and irritable, dressed in plain black. She had once been blonde and pretty. What an odd thing for a scientist to care about: a stranger's perception of her appearance.

Correctly (but with a tinge of regret) she responded with *vous* rather than *tu*: "Yes, it is a lovely evening. Are you attending the presentation here tonight?"

He laughed soundlessly, the effect pleasantly conspiratorial. "No, I usually avoid crowds. But I did hope to meet you tonight. Your tour over here has been on the front page of every newspaper."

"You have the advantage of me, sir. Are you a physician? A scientist?"

"I am merely Marcel. I have no legitimate occupation, so I pass the time playing chess. Would you care for a Gitane?" She glimpsed the familiar blue box he took from his pocket and felt a pang of homesickness.

Ah, to smoke quietly in a garden at twilight with a beautiful young man—what a guilty pleasure. And how long it had been since she had done it. She accepted her cigarette, then watched as he casually lit a match one-handed, striking the head with his thumbnail. The effect of inhaling the smoke was like the effect of his *tu*: Calmness coated her grain of grit as in the creation of a pearl.

Watching her, he smiled and said, "In this country, women of your age don't smoke."

"I know. It's been horribly difficult to abstain, especially when I'm among dozens of men who are smoking."

"Like tonight, inside the great hall there, with their cigars and pipes. I hoped you would need to escape, so I—ah, in English! *I planted myself in this garden to wait for you.*"

Her scientific English did not readily embrace jokes, so she felt herself smile a second too late. "So you know of my work, sir?"

"Yes. Like you, I am interested in rays. I like your subject: the repulsion of attraction, the half-life of desire. Atomic decay as metaphor for the postwar state of the world."

She laughed. "Is that my subject? I've never heard it described that way. But you said you were not a scientist."

"Correct. I'm more interested in bending natural laws than in discovering them."

"Bending? How do you mean, sir?"

"As you bent the law of conservation of energy with your work. And tonight you bend the law of logic by bestowing an instrument used in measuring the invisible, the—what do you call them? Soupçons? Croutons? Bonbons?"

She laughed again. He clearly did know her work, but his manner of discussing it was so airy, so nimble, so different from the oppressive adulation and heavy-browed seriousness she was used to. When was the last time anyone had dared to joke with her? Not even Paul had done so. "Electrons, sir, as I suspect you know very well. And have you a project for your bending of natural law?"

He smiled. "Oh, yes. My project is an attempt to—how can I say this?—depict the half-life of human desire. That is why I am so interested in your decay, or should I say delay. What is the word you have made for it? 'Radioactivity'? Naturally, you have seen such a toy as this." He took from his pocket a short, fat brass cylinder with a glass lens at one end and handed it to her.

She turned the familiar object in her fingers. "A spinthariscope. It

shows the decay through the fluorescence of the alpha particles. Sir William Crookes' accidental discovery."

"Ah, discovered by accident! I'm a great admirer of accidents, of oxidants, of exceedance, of Occidents and Orients. And the lovely name, like *scintillate*. A scintilla of life, of light. But I find the toy more irritating than inspirational: the crackling sound of the particles as they flash, the annoyingly predictable rhythm."

What could he mean? Puzzled, she said, "But there's no sound at all. The activity is perfectly silent. And the flashes are random—no pattern."

He looked away for a moment, exhaling smoke. "Yes, I know these phenomena do not possess an objective existence. But I do hear the crackling and I do see the rhythm, so it doesn't matter."

How could this intelligent man make such an irresponsible statement? "It doesn't matter? Sir, as educated people we must try to learn as much about the universe as we can."

He looked back at her and smiled again. "Must we? I usually find myself doing the opposite of what I 'must' do. It's exhausting. Sometimes I simply can't think what to do next if the next thing must be the unthinkable."

Yes, he was a *blagueur*, a teaser, a joker. Mockingly, she said, "Ah, I sympathize, sir. In that case, your only course of action is to refuse to decide, to ask someone else."

His smile widened. "You understand me perfectly. I shall put my dilemma to you, and you will tell me what to do. And then I shall probably do the opposite of what you say!" They both laughed.

He said, "It is this. I am making a picture—a hilarious picture—into which the viewer will want to enter. But as soon as he tries to do so, the picture will eject him. The repulsion of attraction. The expulsion from the garden, if you will. But I find I cannot do what I want with dead paint on canvas. I want the picture to operate on the viewer's brain in the same way that the spinthariscope does, by creating a sensation of delay, the stage between desire and fulfillment, but—"

She interrupted: "But presumably without the irritation you feel when you use the device."

He laughed his soundless laugh. "No such requirement! If the viewer feels irritated when he looks at my picture, so much the better! Are we not always irritated at the frustration of desire?"

She laughed with him. "Very well, if you insist on the irritation. But then—you are an artist?"

His face became serious, and he said, "Actually, no, I don't insist on the irritation. The viewer's response is his business, not mine. And my business is not art. It is breathing, as is yours. I suppose if I must name my occupation, it is making anti-art. I am trying to create something that is not 'a work of art.'"

"Sir, I don't understand a word you say. But I will ponder your problem."

They smoked in companionable silence, watching the last rays of the setting sun stretch above the garden's brick wall.

The previous week, during her tour of the Standard Chemical Company plant in Pittsburgh, which had refined her precious gram of radium from five hundred tons of carnotite, she had been amazed to see women working in the research laboratory. She had mentioned to Mr. Flannery, her tour guide, that a European company would never hire a woman scientist. His response had been that the women were just as qualified as the men but worked harder and for less money. She thought of her two Nobel Prizes. More qualified than the men.

When Paul had ended their liaison and moved back in with his wife and children, she had told herself it was best for both of them. He would continue teaching at the Sorbonne, perhaps gradually regaining his reputation as a respectable husband and father. And she could devote more attention to her research.

What would it be like to work for Standard? She'd have the most modern research facilities and the best-trained staff in the world, not to

mention a bottomless budget. And no teaching, no distracting lover—just research.

That old fantasy rearing its hopeful head again. Standard would want to use her to its economic advantage. She would not be allowed to publish her future discoveries for the benefit of the scientific community; Standard would patent them as trade secrets. The company (and she) would probably become very wealthy. But she would also have to lend her celebrity to the company—giving interviews, making public appearances, being quoted and photographed for product endorsements. Not so different from what she had to do now, except that her money worries would be over.

And the upheaval of moving, of adjusting to yet another new culture and language? She had already been an expatriate for most of her life; of course she could do it again. Was she too old for a fresh start?

She looked at the stranger's spinthariscope, turning it in her fingers, tapping the nail of her forefinger idly on the lens. "If you want the viewer to fall into your picture, you must put the image behind the picture plane, not in front of it. Instead of canvas, you might use glass." She looked up to see his response.

He smoked silently for a minute, then said, "Glass. Yes, I suppose that could work."

Piqued at his lack of enthusiasm, she continued. "Once, when I went into my laboratory at night, I saw what looked like a far-off city glowing in the dark. It was just the dozens of tubes of radium, of course, but for a moment I thought I saw a city lit up in the night—just as you think you see patterns in the spinthariscope. A trick of the mind, of course, but don't all pictures require a trick of the mind for the viewer to 'see' the picture instead of the paint? If you were to use glass, the viewer would automatically be drawn into the picture, the same way we are drawn outdoors when we look through a window."

His face was thoughtful, unsmiling, looking over her head, but she could see the machinery at work behind his eyes.

Suddenly she threw her half-finished cigarette onto the brick walk and ground it under her shoe. "Oh, how I wish I didn't have to go back in there!"

He looked back at her, his expression pleasant but distant.

"Those people want so much from me! They won't be satisfied until they've eaten me alive and patted their mouths with their expensive linen napkins." She laughed, but she could feel the headache coming on.

His face hardened, and he said, "Why do you feel it is your obligation to satisfy their desires? Do you really believe they want that? The fulfillment of desire is the death of desire, yes? What they truly want—what we all want—is a perpetuation of that desire, a stay of execution. Think of yourself as a bride—Marie, *la mariée*—and of them as your suitors, your grooms, your bachelors. Do these bachelors want consummation? Of course not: *Post coitum omne animal triste est.* We want to want. Desire is the definition of life."

Before she could answer—could she have answered?—Dr. Abbey, her sponsor for the evening, approached them and, nodding curtly to the stranger, put his hand on Marie's arm. Pursued by bachelors, she thought. The doctor said, "Madame, the audience is seated and ready. Will you come in?"

She nodded and moved automatically with him toward the door, turning her head to catch a final glimpse of the interesting young man. He flicked his cigarette butt to the ground and raised his hand in farewell. Then she was inside the building, inside the presentation room, being escorted to the podium accompanied by applause.

Later, after more applause and the questions and the dinner and the flattery and the gifts, as she lay in the strange bed of the house in which she was a guest, she thought of a concert she had attended many years earlier.

She remembered it clearly. The month before, her oldest sister, Zofia, had lain on her bier surrounded by evil-smelling lilies. They had shaved off her long hair during her illness, and her bald head under the

white kerchief had jarred with the frilly white lace dress. How stupid to dress her in lace in January. Mama would never have allowed it, but she herself had died less than a year before. Marie had not been allowed to kiss either one farewell for fear of infection.

Because of all the sadness in the house, Papa thought Marie needed to get out, so he had arranged for one of his students to take her to the concert. Having no evening clothes of her own, she had worn Zofia's dark red satin dress and black velvet cloak. The student (What was his name? No matter.) had been excited about hearing and seeing the famous Paderewski, lion tamer of pianos.

But Marie was more taken by the opening movement of Mozart's nineteenth string quartet. It was so disorienting, so ominous. She had no idea where the music was going, what it meant, not even what key it was in. The dissonance fascinated her, lured her. The cello, voice of darkness. She was a cobra listening to a snake charmer's flute. She was compelled to hear, to try to understand the mystery. Her hands gripped the armrests, her knuckles white. Her spine arched, not touching the back of her seat.

But when the dissonance finally resolved into the C major allegro, the mystery vanished. Her hands relaxed, and she sat back, listening politely.

So what was the connection between that long-ago concert and the strange young man in the garden tonight? What had he said his name was? She had heard so many new names over the past few hours; she couldn't remember. But she remembered his playful physics. His desire to perpetuate desire.

She regretted that she would never see him again. She regretted many things.

Remembering the Gitane she had smoked with him, she inhaled deeply and closed her eyes.

That night she dreamed that she opened her eyes in the attic bedroom of her childhood to see her beautiful sister alive and well, her long blonde hair curling around her shoulders, sitting on the foot of Marie's

bed. Zofia smiled mysteriously as she unwrapped small cakes of pink, white, and yellow. Her fine white linen lap was full of cakes. She popped a cake into Marie's mouth and another into her own. Marie's tongue felt the fluffiness of the cake, the grainy sugar, the comical rotundity of the minute poppy seeds, the tart lemon peel, the dusty cinnamon sprinkled on top. The fullness, the richness of that texture! The sweetness! She opened her mouth for more.

And awoke in the dark with tears on her face.

Many years later, long after Marie died, a famous critic wrote, "One of the twentieth century's most influential works of art, Marcel Duchamp's *La mariée mise à nu par ses célibataires, même (The Bride Stripped Bare by Her Bachelors, Even)*, popularly called 'The Large Glass,' is slowly and inexorably deteriorating. Because of its mysterious construction and delicate condition, conservators say it can never be restored. Each day it decomposes more, as though the infinite projections of the straight lines in the Bachelors' Domain were crossed at right angles with invisible rays, creating sparking intersections of radioactive decay."

THE FACE PHANTOM

Paris, 1929

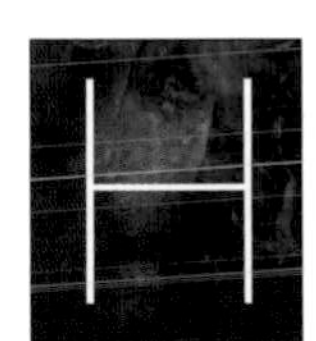
ere's how I would explain her to you: A "face phantom," a medical device used by professors of ophthalmology to give students practice in performing surgery on the human eye. Such surgery necessary for the treatment of cataracts, glaucoma, embedded foreign objects, lack of drainage, and so forth. Manufactured shortly after the Great War, probably around 1920, by Joseph Leiter of Vienna, one of the world's finest makers of medical devices and prostheses. Very expensive, very rare.

Here's what you would see if you looked at her: A life-sized model of a human face and neck mounted on an iron base. Made of thermosetting resin called Bakelite, lightweight and smooth. Features androgynously idealized in a vaguely Roman way, straight nose and small, intelligent mouth. Modeled hair short and choppy, fringed across the forehead and in front of the exposed ears in the "Titus" style of the French Revolution. The back of the head open, the inside hollow, to allow the operator access. The eye orbits empty except that each one contains a large metal spring with prongs along the coil.

Here's what you would see if I demonstrated her to you: The neck is hinged to allow the operator to adjust the horizontal and vertical tilt of the head. The springs in each orbit adjust with screws to allow the operator to affix and position separately each of the two *ex vivo* bovine globes (calves' eyeballs)—in order to simulate as closely as possible the tenuously connected rolling of the human eye in its socket.

Here's what I see when I look at her: My wife, Eulalia. She who transformed my loneliness to joy. My confidante, the receptacle of my passion. My *raison d'être*. The love of my life.

I never wanted to marry until I found Eulalia. A wife seemed a sad commodity, a needless burden. Sagging, aging body; tedious chatter about housekeeping and children; ignorance of and impatience with my intellectual mission, but greed for the money it yields. Repulsive. Erotic desire, fueled by separation and prohibition, would be replaced by familiarity and ennui.

But Eulalia's erotic appeal cannot slacken: She has no body to sag with childbearing, no housekeeping chores to transform her into a drudge. Her stationary image is the projection surface for my erotic fantasies, and her mind reflects my own intellectual prowess. Her head is the external site for all meaning. And I can reveal myself to her fully, with no fear of judgment or betrayal.

In choosing our mates, we seek variation from ourselves, but only slight variation.

My small gifts to Eulalia have always delighted us both. A pair of button earrings depicting golden Siamese dancers on black enamel, nicely sized for her shell-like ears. A felt cloche hat to perch pertly over her short curls. To wrap around her regal neck on cold winter nights, a fox stole with head, paws, and tail; for summer, a long strand of amber beads. And (although the blowsy wives of my colleagues would recoil in horror at

her frank use of paint) lipsticks in colors to accent her floating scarves and feathered bandeaux: Max Factor's Chinese Red with white silk or feathers, Coty's Geranium Magnet with yellow, and Helena Rubenstein's Raspberry Delight with blue and purple. (She never wears black or brown; these drab colors don't flatter her dusky bronze complexion.) I used to paint her mouth into a Cupid's-bow shape (like Clara Bow), but now I paint a more natural hunter's-bow shape (like Joan Crawford).

Tonight's gift will be the best yet. Home at last, I refresh myself with Eau de Cologne, don my dinner jacket, bring our informal supper of wine and fruit to the table, and light the candles. Then I remove her hood and begin what we call our Pygmalion ritual, both of us rejuvenating through kisses. I am tantalized by the flickering candlelight playing over her dark complexion, alternately illuminating and obscuring, so that her face appears to be in motion.

I offer her a strawberry, which she naturally refuses, so I eat it. And then I begin. "My love, I have a wonderful surprise for you."

What is it, what is it? Don't tease! Tell me!

I laugh at her childlike impatience. "All in good time, my dear. If you listen quietly, you will have a lovely reward in a few minutes. If you don't, I may decide to wait until tomorrow night to reveal the surprise."

She responds with charming petulance. *Oh, all right. I shall listen. But don't make me wait too long.*

I smile indulgently at her attempt to control the conversation. We both know that I am always in control. "Very well. Do you remember the paper I wrote this past winter on the possible etiology of Leber's primary optic atrophy? My review of the medical literature had revealed a shocking paucity of case reports, so I presented two of my own cases that were complicated with other central nervous system involvement, and briefly discussed their nosology and relationship to the heredofamilial group of diseases."

Of course I remember. No man ever worked more diligently or with greater dedication to the benefit of humankind. Has your paper finally been accepted for publication?

I bask in her intelligent sympathy. "Even better. I've been invited to present it at this year's International Ophthalmology Conference in Paris. And then it will be published in the conference proceedings."

How wonderful! Your colleagues from all over the world will be able to hear and read your theory. I'm sure the diagnosis and treatment of the disease will be revolutionized because of you. My only regret is that we shall be parted for the duration of your travel to the conference.

Her anxiety pleases me. "Not so, my dear. You will come with me. I will exhibit you at the conference's demonstration of new technologies. Dozens of educated men will admire your beauty and cleverness, all the while oblivious of our secret. It will be a delicious experience for both of us."

Marvelous! I've always wanted to travel with you—and to Paris! Our days will be filled with stimulating and uplifting discourse, and our nights with love. Quel honeymoon!

Her excitement infects me. I quaff the wine, forget the remainder of the fruit, and sweep her off to bed. There I fall upon her, kissing her lips and neck, running one hand over her face while the other pistons between my thighs. The sight that feels, the touch that sees. The boundary between us vanishes. Under my body, her surface becomes warm. The erotic touch unsullied by reminders of disease, pain, and death: She is immortal. My corrupt flesh melts into her perfect substance, bringing us both to that pregnant moment when we blossom into sublimity.

And then we rest, my arm under her head, her face to mine. She breathes through me, and our breathing slows to sleep.

The day after the conference ends, we sit outdoors at Les Deux Magots while I savor my onion tart and creamed coffee. I have taken Eulalia out of her carrying case and set her on the table so she can enjoy the fresh air and the people parading across Saint-Germain-des-Prés.

As we observe the passersby, two voices at a table behind us catch my attention. The primary speaker, with the gravelly voice of a heavy smoker, uses good French but with the rolled *r*'s of a Spaniard. The second voice speaks only rarely—again, French with a Spanish accent, but more languidly than the other. Sometimes the gravelly voice interrupts, impatient to get on with the talk.

I am surprised to hear that the conversation is medical. The voices refer to collective hysteria, dream logic, the birth trauma, the sublimation of sexual paranoia, and other notions that currently preoccupy my Teutonic colleagues. Wanting to discover what sort of gentlemen these might be, I casually shift position so I can glance sidelong at the table whence the voices emanate.

The gravelly voice belongs to a husky young man with an astonishing face: a sensuous mouth that any woman would envy and hooded eyes topped by strongly arched brows. These rather too-feminine features are offset by a barrel torso, strong forearms, and broad hands. The effect is disconcerting, as though a queen's head had been affixed atop a peasant's body.

The languid voice belongs to a slender young gentleman in formal dress. Despite the warm spring day, he wears a black velvet jacket with lapels so broad they overlap the shoulder seams. His shirt is pale blue silk, the cuffs clasped with gold links set with sapphires. (Mind you, this is late morning!) As he listens to his friend speak, he leans back in his chair, chin pointing proudly toward the sky, both slender hands resting on the gold head of his cane.

I have already explained to Eulalia that the city is now a hotbed of painters, sculptors, writers, musicians, and dancers from around the world, all singing the praises of pounding Negro music, paintings with unrecognizable subjects, novels that go nowhere, and other innovations. I am not surprised, then, at her comment: *Despite their medical conversation, they must be artists. Only that would explain the camaraderie between a gangster and a dandy.*

Smiling, I agree: "*D'accord!* An interesting pair. Their project is undoubtedly beyond our comprehension."

At that moment, both young men turn toward us and observe me speaking to Eulalia. After a quick *sotto voce* exchange, they approach our table.

I stand to meet them. The husky one introduces himself, shaking my hand with that melodramatic flourish characteristic of the warmer-climed Continentals. The slender one does not offer his hand but merely gives his name and asks, "May we join you for a moment?" Of course.

Señor Buñuel, the husky one, says, "We are fascinated by your friend here. Its intended purpose is medical? For the study of eyes?"

Pleasantly surprised by his knowledge, I concur.

Señor Dalí, the slender one, says, "But unless I am mistaken, it has another purpose. You—ah—speak to it as you might speak to a lover."

She's alarmed: *He knows!* I say nothing but feel the heat in my face.

The men laugh. Señor Dalí says, "We sympathize. Luis here is a fierce opponent of sexual repression, and I am a walking dictionary of perversions. Yours is agalmatophilia, yes? Erotic love of statues, dolls, and so on. But as a doctor, you must already know that."

Actually, I didn't. And I am disturbed to discover that I belong to a named class, that I am not unique.

Eulalia is incensed: *They think I could be any old statue!* I still cannot speak.

Señor Buñuel says, "Don't worry. Our interest in your device is not erotic—we leave that to you. Our interest is aesthetic. We are making a moving picture and would like to borrow your device for a scene or two."

Eulalia wants to hear more. I have told her about *The Jazz Singer, The Four Horsemen of the Apocalypse, The Birth of a Nation, Metropolis,* and other masterpieces of cinematic motion.

Buñuel continues. "We are making a comedy to outrage the intelligentsia, to commit artistic insurrection, to simulate psychological

segmentation with visual montage, to celebrate the absurdism of Langdon and Keaton while parodying the formalism of Fritz Lang and that crew."

Eulalia is dubious: *Perhaps my French is insufficient to the task, but I'm not sure he's saying anything.* I silently agree.

Perceiving my puzzlement, Señor Dalí attempts to clarify: "We plan to seize the audience with hysteria, to expose their secret hypocrisies and leave them to rot in the sun like a dead, fly-infested donkey. To make the experience of watching the film like being raped."

Now she's even more dubious: *Oh, dear.* I feel myself draw back.

Dalí hastens to reassure me. "Please understand: We have nothing against perversion, as I have already said. Our reading of Freud has convinced us that human sexuality encompasses an immense diversity of expression with no 'correct' objective or method of satisfaction. Polymorphous perversity is our slogan. No, our objection is to hypocrisy, to secrecy. We have scripted our protagonist to be burdened with sexual repression, trite bourgeois sentimentality, conventional morality, good manners—all of which we interpret as symptoms of mental illness. Our images will be consciously violent, intended to force the watchers to repudiate the cumbersome, sterile, dusty tyranny of convention. They will be images of barbarous elementary beauty, no decoration, essence rather than refinement, no falsification, the decaying empire of flesh."

That last phrase I definitely understand. It's the reason I need Eulalia: to fantasize for one brief moment that I can slow my advance on that decaying empire.

And she? What does she think? *Interesting, though not completely coherent. Let us hear more.*

So I say, "How would you use the device? She . . . it is valuable and rare, actually irreplaceable, so I wouldn't want . . . it damaged."

The two look at each other and smile. Dalí says, "No, of course not. We wouldn't damage . . . it. We'd actually like to use it for its intended

purpose: to hold an eyeball for surgery. Our opening scene will show a close-up of an eyeball being cut open."

Now we're on familiar ground. She is reassured: *Well, we've certainly done that before. We did it several times at the conference. Let's see how a moving picture is made.*

So I agree: "Well, we leave Paris tomorrow, but we have no plans for tonight. We shall be happy to be of service to you this evening."

At their studio, they let me read the *mise-en-scène* while they set up the lights and camera. The project calls for a bicycle, a book on Vermeer, actors dressed as nuns and priests, dead donkeys, a couple of pianos . . . *Mon Dieu!* To me it seems absurd and chaotic. But since I am unfamiliar with the procedure of making motion pictures, I shall try to keep an open mind.

I have made it clear that no one is to touch Eulalia but me. When the time comes to shoot the scene, I affix the eyeballs as usual in her orbits. Then the horror begins.

I stand ready, scalpel in hand. When Señor Buñuel sees me, he says, "No, no, no. Not the scalpel. Here—use this."

A razor. A straight razor. A cutthroat razor. Weapon of penny-dreadful villains. Sweeney Todd in *The String of Pearls*. The escaped ourang-outang in the preposterous "The Murders in the Rue Morgue." Literary potboilers, dime novels, pulp fiction. Trash for the masses.

I protest. "Señor, this thing is not worthy of my hand. I work with medical instruments, not barbers' tools."

Buñuel is unmoved. "You must use the razor. The symbolism is important. It must be the sharpest, longest, shiniest, most wicked razor possible. Your puny scalpel would barely be seen on the screen."

I fold my arms. "Sir, I cannot. It would be an insult to my profession."

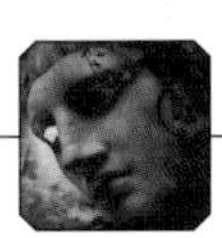

He rips the cigarette from his mouth, stamps it under his foot, and says, "Fine. I'll do it myself. I promise I won't touch your precious phantom any more than necessary."

I'm about to protest when Eulalia interrupts: *Let him do it. I don't mind. Let's finish it.*

I freeze. She has never disagreed with me before. And she has never permitted another man to touch her. *I* have never permitted another man to touch her.

Confused, I say, "Very well. I will set the eyeballs if you wield the razor."

He places his huge left hand on top of her head to steady her during the cut. It looks as though he's pushing her through the floor. Humiliating.

His first gash is so forceful that the eyeball is sliced in two, each half softly plopping to the floor. The scene is ruined and must be filmed again. I choose another calf's eyeball from the ice chips in the bucket and affix it in Eulalia's orbit.

Slash! *Ah, my love!* she sighs. Again the eyeball is ruined. Again I replace it for another try.

Slash! *Oh, my heart!* Again. Again.

But as he brings the razor up for the next attempt, I see it all.

She is speaking to him, not me. To those peasant hands savaging her eyes. To that violence, that blood, that corruption.

And he is doing it on purpose. Again and again. So his young, virile blood can flow into her, revivifying her, owning her.

I remember her words: *Let's finish it.*

Very well. It is finished.

I turn toward the door. She has one chance to call me back.

Dalí says, "Señor?" I don't answer.

Buñuel says, "Señor?" I don't answer.

And then I hear her. *Go, then. Leave me with him.*

LEPER ARRESTED IN ICE CREAM SCAM

Rural Louisiana, 1949

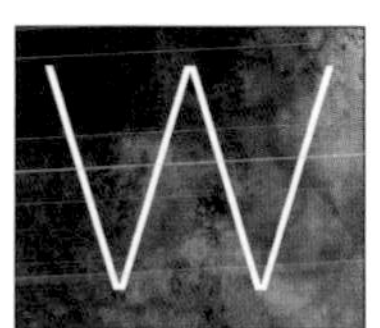

hen Goose first saw that Mergenthaler Linotype, you could have knocked his eyes off with a stick. A machine six feet wide and seven feet tall, weighing around three thousand pounds! As if Pa's old Diamond T pickup had reared up on its hind end to beg like a ginormous coonhound. The Linotype had thousands of moving metal parts clacking and clicking, like clocks all keeping different times. And around the machine was this enticing smell of hot lead and fresh newsprint and sticky black printer's ink. The signs blared *Danger! Danger!*

Goose was magnetized. He felt like he was falling right into that clattering Linotype. Falling in love. He didn't realize that he'd gotten too close until he felt Mr. Sol's hand on his shoulder pull him back. Then Mr. Sol put his mouth next to Goose's ear and shouted, "Our type compositor is so fast he can hang a line of type before the last line is ejected. On good days he composes at ten thousand ems per hour." Goose had no idea what that meant. But he knew he wanted to *be* that man, that king, the master of that noisy metal monster.

The type compositor, a tall, muscular man with a dark crew cut, perched lightly on a swiveling stool. His blue cotton work shirt had the sleeves cut off at the shoulders, so Goose could see the tattoos on his sweating biceps. One tattoo had the letters "USMC" under an American eagle standing on a purple heart (a Purple Heart!), and the other had "Semper Fi" under a cartoon bulldog chomping a cigar and wearing a spiked collar. His hands were all over that machine, doing everything at once, like those Hindu gods with all the arms. No wasted motion. He and the machine had clearly been dancing together for a long, long time.

That man could not be a patient at the leprosarium. Operating a Linotype was too dangerous for people with Hansen's disease. If they got burned or cut, they wouldn't feel pain. Then they'd get infected and need amputations. So this was somebody else—somebody who didn't scare easy, who didn't mind working in a leprosarium, who knew that Hansen's could be contracted only in childhood.

The man was so busy that he didn't realize Mr. Sol and Goose were watching him. Mr. Sol waited until the man paused in his work and turned to toss the line slugs into the hellbox for remelting. Then Mr. Sol rolled forward in his wheelchair and put his hand on the man's arm to let him know he had company.

The man turned around, and Mr. Sol introduced him. "Begay, this young man wants to learn the Linotype business. Meet Waylon Beaufort Boudreaux, called Goose for his amazing gooseberry-green eyes."

Goose opened his mouth in greeting, but nothing came out. The man looked neither white nor colored, so Goose didn't know how to address him. *Sir, mister, boss, brother,* what? Goose waited for the clue to come from the man's mouth: *Boy* or *child* or *son* would tip him off.

As Goose had gotten familiar with the leprosarium, his amazement at the patients' symptoms had been overtaken by amazement at their colors. The doctors and most of the nurses were white, of course, but the patients were all the colors of the world. One man was very pale pink; one lady was so dark that her skin reflected shimmering blue light. There were people from Barbados, Hawaii, Nigeria, Morocco, Honduras, and a dozen other places. Mr. Sol had given Goose a world map to tack up on the wall in the leprosarium's social room so folks could stick pins in the places they were from, and that map bristled.

Even more astonishing than the colors of the patients was their disregard of those colors. Sure, they divided themselves up by similarities: ladies with other ladies, or Spanish-speaking folks, or giggling adolescents. But they never divided up by color. Dark and light folks routinely ate lunch with each other and sat talking together in the social room. When Goose had asked Mr. Sol about this, he laughed and said, "Well, we're probably in the only place in Louisiana where something trumps race. It's just too bad that something has to be Hansen's disease."

Now, when Mr. Sol noticed that Goose was puzzled about how to address the man at the Linotype, he said, "Begay here comes from the big Navajo reservation in the Southwest."

So. A red Indian. Goose had never seen one in person. Never given them much thought. They existed in picture books, history books. Most of them lived on the other side of the country, which might as well have been the other side of the moon.

Begay. Strange name. First or last name? Did he have only one name? Goose still didn't know how to address him. Was a red Indian an honorary white person or an honorary colored person?

The man stuck out his hand and shook Goose's, squeezing. Goose's finger bones compressed uncomfortably. The man said, "Pleasure, kid," and nodded, looking through slits so narrow that Goose couldn't even see what color the eyes were. Begay didn't smile, so that was like a white man.

Kid. That was a new one. Goose played it safe. "*Bonjour*, boss."

The man lowered his eyebrows and looked at Mr. Sol, who said, "Just call him Begay, Goose. Not boss. He's been a type compositor for fifteen years, since he was about your age. He was wounded at Henderson Field on Guadalcanal, but his main job was sending and receiving coded messages. Came here after the war to help me start up *The Argus*."

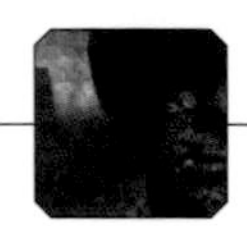

Now Goose knew how to talk to the man. Everyone liked to tell war stories. He had already milked Pa dry and all the other veterans he met, including the ones in the leprosarium. So he was confident of a friendly reception when he said, "Honored to meet a war hero, sir. I'd love to hear about your time at Guadalcanal."

But those eyebrows went down again. Begay shook his head and said, "Nope. No stories."

Goose didn't know what that meant. Did the man have no stories to tell? Did he have stories but not want to tell them? Did he just not like Goose? Goose took a step backward, rebuffed, feeling stupid. He learned later on that Begay had a reputation around the leprosarium for not talking much. Maybe something had happened in the war to make him like that, or maybe he'd always been like that.

Mr. Sol eased the awkward silence by asking Begay if Goose could sit and watch him work for a bit. Begay looked at Goose pretty hard for a minute, eyebrows down, no smile, and then nodded.

That night after Pa signed the paper giving his permission for Goose to work in the leprosarium's print shop, he handed it to Goose and said, "What is it, child?"

Goose inhaled and said, "It's—well, it's the boss. I think he thinks I'm a dog that won't hunt."

Pa laughed and said, "If he didn't want you, you wouldn't be going to work for him." But Goose looked at the floor.

So Pa said, "Child, liking or not liking folks ain't as important as you might think. What's important is everybody working together to get the job done. Your boss was in the war, so he knows that. You work as hard as you can for the next four years, and then you won't ever have to see him again. You learn and you stay out of his way, then you'll be a journeyman printer and have your pick of jobs. Better'n driving a truck like me."

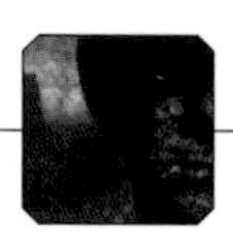

Goose raised his head and nodded. He *would* do it.

All the work in a print shop is dirty, but Goose began with the dirtiest. Mr. Sol told him the name for the job he was doing was printer's devil. A lot of famous folks had done this same job when they were young: Benjamin Franklin, Thomas Jefferson, Mark Twain, even President Harding. Mr. Sol said that the very first printer's devil was from Africa, a colored boy (like Goose!) who worked in Italy a long time ago. So Goose learned to mix ink and fetch type, to take slugs from the hellbox to be melted and recast, and to clean up stray squirts and spills of lead. Begay didn't make many of those squirts and spills, but when they did happen, Goose wondered whether he had maybe done them on purpose. Just to show Goose who was who.

Begay aside, Goose liked the job. He kept busy doing different things and getting to know the folks who came in and out of the print shop and the newspaper office. He especially liked Miz Satou, a young lady from the Philippines. She was Mr. Sol's typist, and she could operate her keyboard almost as fast as Begay could operate his. Miz Satou did have Hansen's disease. She still had all her fingers and toes, but her eyebrows were gone, and her nose was pretty flat. (When people with Hansen's didn't get the sulfa drugs in time, their faces got to look like lions' faces. That's why the patients called their baseball team the Lions. A joke.) But she wore bright red lipstick and perfume anyway.

Mr. Sol told Goose that Miz Satou had saved the lives of a bunch of American soldiers by carrying secret messages across Japanese lines. When the patients heard that she couldn't get good medical treatment in the Philippines, that she was lying on a bamboo mat on a dirt floor all day, they ganged together and took up a collection to get her to Louisiana.

Now, Goose got on famously with ladies of any color. They always told him how smart he was and how pretty his eyes were and so forth. But he particularly liked Miz Satou because she was a lady *and* a war hero. Unlike Begay, she was happy to tell Goose her war stories. Whenever he could, he brought her a few pecan pralines to sweeten the conversation.

But if he saw her taking a smoke break with Begay, he waited until later. It riled him the way they put their heads together. The way they smiled. Begay never smiled at him.

Goose's favorite part of the job was learning to operate the Linotype. Mr. Sol said Goose was a natural for the job, and Goose reckoned it was so. He was particular with his fingers, fast and careful, and he knew his punctuation. And when he was setting type, that's all he could see. You could explode a cherry bomb right behind him and he wouldn't flinch.

And he could spell. He'd won his elementary school spelling bee two years running. Usually the school gave the winner a dictionary as a prize. But since they'd already given Goose the dictionary in the fifth grade, they had to give him a thesaurus in the sixth grade. Goose still loved both books. Sometimes, he'd stick a finger into one and try to memorize the page it landed on. On the rare occasions when he wasn't sure how to spell a word, he wrote it out, either on paper or with his finger in the air. When he could see the word, he could always tell whether it was supposed to be *privilege* or *priviledge*, *independent* or *independant*. Writing a word out took a few seconds, but that didn't matter in school.

It did matter for the Linotype work. And Begay never had to write words out to know how to spell them. He . . . just . . . knew. Always.

Goose worked like a dog. Within a year, he had achieved a best speed of seven thousand ems per hour. (Now he knew that an em was a unit of measurement the width of a capital M.) That was lickety-split, especially for a beginner, and Mr. Sol often told Goose what a great type compositor he was getting to be.

But Begay never complimented Goose. And Begay continued to work at a best speed of ten thousand ems per hour.

Goose managed to follow Pa's advice and keep out of Begay's road until one morning: Boom! Goose's ears rang, and orange flames swarmed up the front of the Linotype. Goose sat like a bump on a log, staring at the blaze.

Then Begay was running toward Goose faster than any big man

had a right to run, and Goose felt an impact like he'd been hit by Pa's truck. Begay dropped him ten feet away and ran back toward the fire to cut the fuel supply and the pressure. Miz Satou hustled in from the editorial office and sprayed the Linotype with the chemical fire extinguisher.

Three minutes later, the ruckus was all over. Goose learned that a gasket in one of the fuel pipes connected to the Linotype had given way and a spray of gasoline had shot out, igniting the machine's metal heater. He started to shiver when he realized that Begay and Miz Satou had saved Mr. Sol's precious newspaper office. Maybe saved the leprosarium. All the doctors and nurses and medical equipment. The two hundred patients who lived there.

And Begay had saved Goose. Saved his life.

Unbelievably, Begay and Miz Satou were standing there laughing. Their faces and hands and clothes were black and oily—but they were laughing. And then they looked at Goose, and Miz Satou said, "Are you all right?"

Goose's teeth were chattering. They were heroes, and he was a coward. A yellow dog.

He waved his hand at them, turned away, and walked down the hall. Left the building and stood there in the sunshine for a minute. Walked the two miles home and took to his bed. When Pa got home that evening and asked how his day had been, he said fine. He also said he was tuckered out and needed to stay home for the next day or two. He didn't mention the fire.

The Linotype wasn't damaged. It just needed cleaning up. So three days later, when Goose came back to work, there was Begay, setting type at ten thousand ems per hour, like always. He and Goose nodded to each other, and then Goose began quietly emptying the hellbox.

That's when Goose started to listen to the rumors about Begay, rumors whispered by the town's porch-sitters. Goose used to just wave at these folks as he made his weekly rounds, but now he stopped to natter and let the conversation come around to Begay. He heard that Begay had

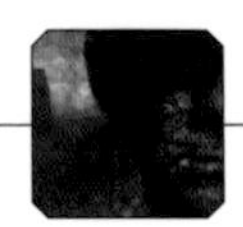

left a wife and children behind. Begay was a souse . . . on the lam . . . a no-account. Goose held tight to the rumors.

Because Mr. Sol now had two type compositors, he was able to change *The Argus* from a monthly newspaper to a weekly. And Goose got Pa to give away copies as he made his deliveries around town. That way, the townies learned about the leprosarium—learned that the patients were just folks, not rabid cannibalistic zombies. Some of the ladies from the white and colored churches began to visit, bringing in old clothes to give away and baskets of cookies and jellies and suchlike. When Mr. Sol told Goose what a difference Pa's deliveries had made in the townsfolks' attitude toward the patients, he said, "Goose, if my tear ducts still worked, I'd weep for joy," and they both laughed.

Later that year, Mr. Sol's health took a turn for the worse. His skin lesions got more painful, his breathing got louder, and his fingers curled in, like claws. He hated to do it, but he had to cut back on the newspaper work. Miz Satou got other patients to write some of the articles, and she and Goose wrote a few themselves.

What Mr. Sol did when he was feeling punk was to wheel into the social room where there was this old Wurlitzer radio. He'd listen to music and news and especially baseball games. That was his big thing, baseball. He loved to tell baseball stories, like about how he saw President Wilson throw out the first ball to open the 1916 season and how Babe Ruth hit twenty-nine home runs in 1919. Mr. Sol was only a kid when he saw these things, but he remembered them like they'd happened yesterday.

It wasn't only the score, he said. It was the sound of the bat cracking the ball and the way the new grass and fresh air smelled after you'd been cooped up inside all winter and the way everybody sang "Take Me Out to the Ball Game," all swaying together side by side. And the ice cream. Although the song says peanuts and Cracker Jack, Mr. Sol had never eaten that junk. What he did was wait for the ice cream guy to come around during the seventh-inning stretch. That guy rode a tall tricycle that pulled a freezer cart and had an umbrella over it and a silver bell with a long chain that he pulled to ring it. The cones were different then, bigger and made with a lot more sugar, not these modern dinky things that fall apart after one bite and taste like crunchy air. Mr. Sol never got chocolate or strawberry, always vanilla. He said that people who think vanilla doesn't taste like much haven't had the real thing, and he felt sorry for them.

Now, even though relations between the townies and the patients were improving, relations between the patients and the businesses weren't. The food companies were especially afraid of doing business with the leprosarium. Didn't want word to get around that they served lepers, or people might think their equipment was contaminated or some such flapdoodle. Co-Cola refused to deliver to the leprosarium for years, until Pepsi came around, and then Co-Cola did it. But both companies let the patients have only the chipped bottles, which weren't going to be used again.

No one had ever agreed to deliver ice cream.

Goose decided it was time. There was an important game coming up on June 12, and Mr. Sol would surely listen to it on the old Wurlitzer: the Brooklyn Dodgers and the Cincinnati Reds. Goose was determined that Mr. Sol and everyone else would have ice cream for that game. He wanted the whole shebang: ice cream, waffle cones, and a day's rental of a freezer cart that he could pedal around the social room. He'd get Miz Satou, who knew origami, to fold him one of those ice cream hats.

Goose spread the word around the leprosarium that he was making a surprise for Mr. Sol and needed folks to help him out with whatever cash they could spare. Most everyone pitched in, some a little, some a lot, all in change and small bills. Goose had never organized a shindig like this before. One of the patients joked that Goose was moving faster than a one-legged leper in a butt-kicking contest. There was a lot of hoo-ha and shushing and whispering and giggling, but it all happened while Mr.

Sol was listening to the radio or snoozing, so he never suspected. Goose was so busy he never did get around to asking Begay for a donation or telling him about the party.

Since no ice cream company would send one of their precious freezer trucks to the town of Belleville if they knew Pa was going to drive it out to the leprosarium, Goose had to pretend to send a purchase order from a rural business. The ice cream company's driver would bring the truck to the vacant lot behind the Belleville grocery store, then set a spell in the diner to eat his lunch while Pa took over the driving for the rural route. Standard procedure. Only the local drivers knew those muddy back roads.

Goose decided on a malt shop. What should he call it? Milkshakes and More? Ice Cream Heaven? Floats and Fun? He decided on Solly's Sodas—in honor of Mr. Sol, of course. For the delivery address, he used the grocery store, like Pa said other companies did.

One of Pa's sayings that Goose didn't much like was "You're a smart boy school-wise, but sometimes you don't got the sense God gave a monkey wrench." So what if printing up a fake purchase order was against the law? If the company got its money, what was the harm?

When the big day came and Mr. Sol was in the social room fiddling with the knobs of the Wurlitzer to get it tuned right, all the other patients and the doctors and nurses snuck into the hall to hide. Ten minutes before the first pitch, Goose made his entrance, feeling as tall and important as Rex the Mardi Gras king. He pedaled into the room on that grand tricycle with Miz Satou's origami ice-cream hat on his head, clanging the bell and singing out, "Mr. Sol, will you have vanilla as usual?"

Then everyone crowded into the room laughing and cheering and yelling flavors out: Strawberry! Chocolate! Vanilla! Strawnilla! Chocoberry! Vanolate! And they danced around Mr. Sol's wheelchair, using feet, crutches, wheels, whatever they had. In all the uproar, Mr. Sol's mouth opened like he wanted to speak, but nothing came out.

So Goose said, "Well, sir, I take it that's a yes!" and put a grand sugary waffle cone with two scoops of vanilla into Mr. Sol's hand. And Mr. Sol opened his mouth and took a little lick like he wasn't sure what to do. But then he definitely remembered what to do: He took a big bite and closed his eyes and groaned, "Oh, no, my head!" And everyone laughed again and cheered for Mr. Sol's first ice cream headache in thirty years, then crowded round to get their own cones. Of course, Goose offered ice cream again during the seventh-inning stretch, and everyone got as full as a tick and didn't want supper. And that ice cream tasted just as good as those twenty runs that the Dodgers scored against the Reds that day.

During the party, whenever Goose noticed Miz Satou looking around for Begay, he turned his head to look somewhere else.

The headline of the next morning's *Belleville Bugle* read "LEPER ARRESTED IN ICE CREAM SCAM."

When Miz Satou handed him the article, Goose's stomach lurched up into his craw. First, the word "leper." Just as nasty as the word "nigger." A hating word. Terrible word for a newspaper to print. And anyway, Begay wasn't a patient. Second, Goose had never meant to scam anyone. He'd handed over the money for the ice cream fair and square. Third . . . well, Begay. And him a wanted man.

He wasn't Goose's favorite person, but without him *The Argus* might fold. And that newspaper was really important. Mr. Sol used it to help the patients understand their disease better, but he also used it to connect them with the world outside, running articles on the war and the World Series and Hollywood. And it was because of that newspaper that the leprosarium finally got the sulfa drugs, the post office, the telephone, the paved road, and so on. Even the vote. Until a few years before, people with Hansen's couldn't vote. It had really burned Mr. Sol how with Hansen's you weren't only sick, you were punished by the law for being sick, like a criminal.

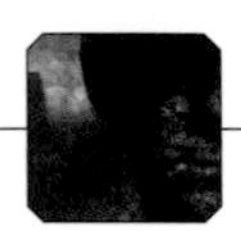

As Miz Satou looked out the window with her arms folded tight, Goose read the article and realized his mistake. He'd collected the money and given it to Pa to hand over to the Carvel driver. Pa had kicked a bit—he wasn't used to handling money—but Goose had convinced him that as long as the company got paid, everything would be hunky-dory. (He hadn't told Pa about the fake purchase order.) But after Pa had driven off to deliver the ice cream to the leprosarium, the article said, the Carvel driver got to wondering. Why cash? Businesses always paid with checks. And those checks got mailed to the company's finance office, not handed to a driver. So instead of going to the diner to eat his lunch like he was supposed to, the Carvel driver had gone into the grocery store to show the manager the purchase order and ask about this Solly's Sodas place.

After that, things had happened pretty fast. Begay was arrested in the print shop, right about the time of the first pitch. He'd spent the night in jail.

While Goose was reading, Mr. Sol rolled his wheelchair into the office. The disease had turned his face, like Miz Satou's, into a lion's face. Just now it looked mighty fierce. He said, in a thick, heavy voice that Goose had never heard before, "I think there's been a mistake here, don't you?" And he looked real hard at Goose.

Goose's face was hot. He said, "Well . . . I . . . well . . . but he's a . . . wanted man. Isn't he?"

Mr. Sol lowered his lion's forehead. "Oh, you heard about that, did you? Do you know the details?" Goose shook his head, and Mr. Sol said, "Kurumi? Please tell Goose the story."

Miz Satou's voice was low and sad. "Begay is wanted for assault and escaping arrest. While he was away at the war, another man moved into his house and took over his wife and kids. Where Begay comes from, the women own everything, the houses and livestock and all. So he returned from the war and found no wife, no children, no home, no nothing."

Goose tried to imagine how he'd feel if he went home one day to find that Pa had taken in another boy. Had given that boy all of Goose's

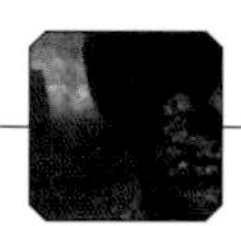

clothes and books and other things. Had said that he didn't want Goose around no more. It was such an ugly thought that he closed his eyes to shut it out. His breath came quick and shallow as he listened to Miz Satou say the rest. "He didn't know what to do, so he went on a bender—the only time in his life he ever got drunk. Then he returned and tried to stab his wife's new man with a pocketknife. The man was only scratched. When the tribal police came to arrest him, he ran."

Mr. Sol was still looking pretty fierce when he said, "So, Goose, I think you'll agree that this isn't quite the same situation that we have here, is it? Not the same thing as intent to defraud and commit larceny, is it?"

Goose's head, eyes closed, lowered.

Mr. Sol's voice softened a bit, and he put a hand on Goose's arm. "Do you need to take off work this morning to go see Sheriff Cooley?"

Goose held quiet a minute. Pa and Mr. Sol and Miz Satou had been so proud of him. And he had worked so hard to learn type composing. It hurt to open his eyes, but he inhaled and did it and looked at Mr. Sol. "Yes, sir. I do."

Mr. Sol's face was friendly again. He squeezed Goose's arm and said, "Well, you might want to walk into his office on your own power. You don't want him knocking on your pa's door." Goose closed his eyes again and nodded.

Begay had surely figured it all out by now and told the sheriff anyway. Goose might as well get it over with. Do it and don't be dreadin' it. That's what Pa always said.

Sheriff Cooley looked up from writing at his desk. "What's up, boy? You need something?"

Goose took a breath, gave his name and address, explained that he worked at the leprosarium's print shop, used all the sirs he had, and confessed.

Sheriff Cooley didn't react like Goose expected him to. First off, he smiled at Goose and said, "So you're a Boudreaux? You must be Jackson's boy. I've knowed your pa since we was kids. Good driver, Jackson. Finds his way into and out of all the hellacious holes we got around here."

Now humbled below Pa in addition to being humbled below Begay and Mr. Sol and Miz Satou, Goose looked at the ground and waited to be arrested.

But the sheriff's surprises weren't finished. He raised his eyebrows and said, "Look here, son. I don't know what's got into you, but we already know who done it. Mr. Begay done signed a confession."

Goose's eyes widened. "But . . ." Silence.

The sheriff looked at him curiously.

Goose said, "May I speak to Begay—to Mr. Begay for a minute, sir?"

"Sure. No reason why not. I'll take you in directly."

Sheriff Cooley escorted Goose upstairs to the holding cell. Begay was sitting on the bunk in the cell, his back against the wall, smoking one of Sheriff Cooley's hand-rolled. When he saw the two come in, he nodded politely and said, "Nice smooth shag, Sheriff." That was the first time Goose ever heard Begay speak without he was spoken to first.

The second time was when Begay looked at Goose and said, "Kid, I've already got a rap sheet. You don't. Let's keep it that way."

Goose was thunderstruck.

After Begay was extradited to Arizona, Goose was the only type compositor for *The Argus*. The newspaper didn't fold, but Mr. Sol did have to cut it back again to a monthly. Goose worked hard and kept his nose clean and earned more money than Pa ever had. And everyone said they were proud of him.

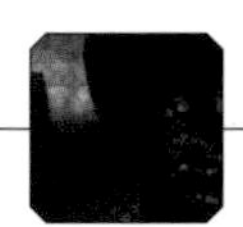

It should have made him happy, and it mostly did. But there was this black lump in his chest a lot of the time.

He asked Pa what would happen to Begay, and Pa said, "I don't know, child. He's got to work things out with his own folks in his own way."

He asked Mr. Sol what would happen to Begay, and Mr. Sol said, "I don't know, Goose. He'll probably be all right. He's a resourceful fellow."

Goose didn't feel any better after these conversations. He didn't ask Miz Satou. Didn't want to make her feel bad by mentioning it.

About a month after Begay left, Miz Satou came into the newspaper office waving three picture postcards and saying, "Gentlemen! Take a break!" Mr. Sol put down his blue editing pencil and Goose swiveled his stool away from his work and left the Linotype purring. Goose and Miz Satou crowded round Mr. Sol's desk so they could see the cards.

The card addressed to Miz Satou showed a black-and-white cartoon of a tall cactus under a night sky with a full moon and lots of stars. A hammock slung from two of the cactus's arms held a sleeping man whose legs sprawled over the sides of the hammock and whose open mouth emitted a string of Zs. A smaller hammock held a long-eared jackrabbit emitting a string of smaller Zs. A buzzard perched on top of the cactus like a Christmas-tree angel, and a steer skull sat on the ground below. The caption read: "At the end of the trail." On the back of the card was a one-cent stamp postmarked Chinle, Arizona. In the message space, in handwriting so forceful it indented the card, was just one word: *Begay*.

Miz Satou said, "Well, he's home, anyway." She smiled at Goose and Mr. Sol, and Goose felt the black lump in his chest melt a bit.

The card addressed to Mr. Sol showed a mountain lion sitting on a boulder against a blue sky crossed by a bright rainbow. The lion's massive round paws looked the size of dinner plates. Its tawny neck was stretched long, its black-backed ears were flattened, and its black-lined eyes were closed. Its mouth was opened wide to show the pink tongue and knifelike

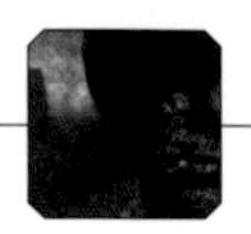

incisors. But it wasn't growling or yawning. It looked like . . . was it singing? It couldn't be, of course. But that's what it looked like. Written in the message space in the same forceful handwriting was the same single word: *Begay*.

Mr. Sol laughed. "This lion is absolutely me! Having a great day! The best portrait I'll ever have!" Goose and Miz Satou laughed with him. Goose's black lump melted a bit more.

The postcard addressed to Goose was captioned "Spider Rock, Canyon de Chelly National Monument." It looked like no landscape Goose had ever seen. No buildings, no people, no animals, no water, no trees, no grass, no flowers. The horizon was flat as a table, with a cloudy sky pressing down like it weighed more than the earth. Enormous anvil-shaped rocks, layered like red and white flapjacks, jutted up to that sky. A few dry greenish-gray shrubs huddled against the base of the rocks. One skinny, lonely dirt road wandered through the picture like it was so lost it couldn't even find itself.

And in the center of the photograph stood a tall, tall rock split vertically down the middle, half of it a bit shorter than the rest. Like a man standing next to a boy—not touching, but together. Facing in the same direction.

Goose was expecting the same *Begay* in his message space as on the other cards. But instead, there were three different words: *Beshiltheeni—Metal Master*.

With Mr. Sol's help, Goose sounded it out: *bay-sheelt-hay-ay-nee*.

Did Begay have a first name after all? A secret name, never to be spoken? A nickname, like Goose? Or was this a title he was handing on?

Whatever it was, Goose had it now. Metal Master. Now he needed to get back to work to earn it. Ten thousand ems per hour.

Plus one.

DO NOT FEED

Tucson, 1970

amn. Brad hadn't cleaned the room after they killed the dogs last night.

Erlinda uncoiled the hose from its reel on the wall and began washing down the double-decker rows of stainless-steel cages. Because the dogs had fasted for a day before their fatal sodium pentobarbital injections, most of the cages contained no vomit or feces, just the odd tuft of fur or puddle of urine.

She was glad the gastro experiment was over. Abdominal surgery was pretty hard on the dogs. They worried and fussed with the black sutures across their bellies, sometimes ripping them out. Erlinda's worst experience on the job had happened with one of the gastro dogs, a pretty white Spitz. When Erlinda had walked in on the morning after the surgery, the dog was standing in her cage, shivering with cold and fright, her teeth chattering. Erlinda blinked, processing what she was looking at. During the night, the dog had somehow torn out all the stitches. Her entire incision had unzipped, and her wet intestines lay mounded like spaghetti on the cage floor.

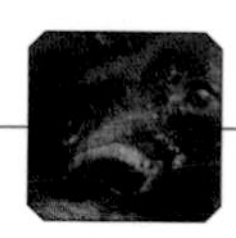

Erlinda had quickly prepared a lethal injection and raced to put the Spitz out of her misery. As the dog sank to the floor of her cage and expired, Erlinda had felt her own breath explode in relief.

Now she hosed and squeegeed the floor and wiped the sink down. The room was clean, ready for the new experiment, something to do with lead poisoning. The dogs for the experiment—all puppies this time—would arrive this morning. Erlinda mentally rehearsed the intake procedure as she carried the cleaning equipment out of the room.

Up on the loading dock, Stan would take the carriers from the shelter's van, stack them in the freight elevator, and send them down to the basement. Erlinda, Tony, and Lollie would remove the cages from the elevator, stack them on the dolly, and roll them to the intake room. There, Lollie would open the cages one by one. Tony would remove and restrain each puppy while Erlinda injected it. When the sedative took effect, Erlinda would use the electric clippers around the pup's anus, mouth, and ears. Lollie's hand would plunge into the pup's throat to cut its vocal cords with a biopsy punch. And Tony would clamp its left ear in the tattoo pliers. Finally, Erlinda and Tony would lift the sleeping pup, submerge it momentarily in the pyrethrin bath, and put it back into its carrier. Lollie would then swing the carrier back onto the dolly.

The intake procedure usually went pretty smoothly. There was only that one time when Erlinda had underestimated the amount of ketamine needed for a big red dog, long-nosed and prick-eared. The dog had awakened while submerged in the tick bath and had clamped onto Erlinda's arm in fright. Tony had immediately labeled the dog a biter and wanted to put him down. But Erlinda had intervened to save him, so he'd been assigned to the arthritis experiment room. Later, she had secretly taken him on as her special favorite, giving him extra exercise and food. In her mind, she called him Zorro, the fox. They weren't supposed to name the lab animals. Avoid emotional attachments.

After all the pups were processed, they'd be taken to the new experiment room (now clean, thanks to her) and unloaded into their

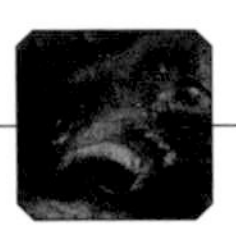

permanent cages. They'd sleep for a few hours, drying in the heat from the vents, and wake up to fresh food and water. Today's process would be easier than usual because the animals would be pups rather than adults. Not only were puppies more lightweight and submissive, they adapted to cage life more easily than adults.

Still, it was a hard thing to think of puppies living their whole lives in cages, under fluorescent lights. Never seeing the sun. Never running full-tilt across a vacant lot to jump and catch a Frisbee in midair. And God knew what the experiment would do to them, but Erlinda didn't. She didn't know much about lead poisoning.

Ah, well. They'd have a better life here in the lab than on the streets. Well, safer, anyway. Of course, safer wasn't the same as better. Still, it was a lot. And people would benefit from the medical research.

Erlinda shook her head. Get on with it.

As she was putting the cleaning equipment away in the hall closet, she heard a voice: "Linda? Erlinda Tapia?"

Turning, she blinked and registered the tall white lab coat, the generously made-up black eyes. The woman seemed familiar, but Erlinda couldn't place her. "Yes?"

The tall woman grinned and stuck out her hand. "Ceci Ortiz. I used to help your brother work on that Chevy Impala. Did he ever get that thing running?"

Now she remembered. Skinny Ceci, Leo's friend. Mom had called her the bottomless pit because she was always hungry. She had been at their house nearly every day after school for a couple of years. Mom had occasionally mended her ripped jeans. Nice kid, quiet. That must have been—what?—seven or eight years ago? Yeah, that's right; Ceci had come home with Leo the day school let out early because Kennedy had been shot.

They shook hands. Erlinda said, "Yes, it runs. It's gorgeous. Beautiful hundred-spoke rims that he paid a fortune for. Not that he ever drives it." They laughed. Low riders were for the occasional stately parade, not for mundane transportation. "What are you doing here?"

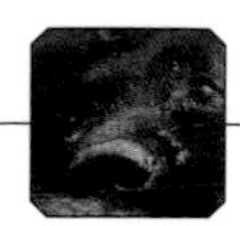

"I'm the researcher for the lead toxicity experiment." Erlinda glanced at the name tag on the lab coat and felt her eyes widen: *Cecilia Paz Ortiz, M.D.* She had heard that Ceci had gotten some kind of scholarship, but hadn't known about med school. "I was told you would be my lab tech, so I wanted to come and talk to you about the experiment. Can I buy you lunch today?"

Erlinda smiled. No other doctor had ever done this. "Ceci, researchers are supposed to treat lab techs as peons, not as colleagues. You don't ask me, you order me."

They laughed again. "Okay, I order you to have lunch with me today. Noon in the cafeteria?"

Erlinda smiled and nodded.

"Great. See you then." Ceci turned and walked away.

A barrio *chica* who had finished med school at twenty-five. Impressive.

"*¿Linda, por qué está mi azarcón en la basura? Tengo el empacho.*" Erlinda's mother picked the plastic bag of bright orange powder out of the trash can.

Erlinda, on all fours, kept pulling things out of the under-sink cupboard, quickly dividing them into piles on the kitchen floor: Keep, toss, ask Ceci. She didn't look up at her mother as she worked. "Speak English, Mom. You know you need the practice. And put that junk back in the trash. Use something else for your indigestion."

"But Rita says—"

"I don't care what your sister says. Look, I know you've got some aches and pains. So stop smoking. Stop drinking coffee. Stop eating chilis. See a doctor. But I won't let you swallow that poison anymore."

Mom sighed, dropped the bag back into the trash can, and looked around at the mess on the kitchen floor. "What are you doing?"

"I'm getting rid of all the lead-based crap in this house. Old paint

cans, old newspapers, Leo's old fishing sinkers. And these!" Erlinda held up a handful of Bolirindo lollipops, the sweet treats that Tía Rita always brought for Leo's twins when she flew in from El Paso. "Mom, these things are death on a stick!" She hurled the candies into the trash can. "Disgusting!"

Mom smiled slightly, turned to leave the kitchen, and said, "Okay, *jita*. You go right ahead and save the world. I'll be digging weeds." She headed for the back door.

Erlinda looked after her. "Oh, Mom! Don't be like that. This is really important. Ceci says—"

Mom's voice sounded distantly: "Ceci says, Ceci says. Ceci the big-shot doctor. Ceci the bottomless pit."

Erlinda pursed her lips and returned to her important work.

That weekend, the after-dinner activity at Mom's split into the usual factions. Erlinda's brothers, Leo and Lorenzo, went out to the back yard to smoke and talk about cars, jobs, and sports. Mom chatted with Leo's wife, Valerie, as the two of them worked in the kitchen, washing the dishes and wrapping up a mountain of leftovers to go home with Valerie and Leo. In the living room, Erlinda played and sang with Leo's boisterous twins. Occasionally Valerie yelled from the kitchen, "Keep it down to a roar in there!"

Deanna and Teresa had been babbling and stringing sounds together long before their first birthday. By their second birthday, they were making complete sentences in English and Spanish (and Spanglish, which Valerie tried to discourage, though Erlinda thought it was funny). By their third birthday, their vocabularies had exploded into hundreds of words. Now, at four, they sang songs they learned from the radio and mimicked the speech of adults behind their backs. Like their parents, they had spoken both languages from the beginning, so switching was no harder than walking from one room to another—probably even easier,

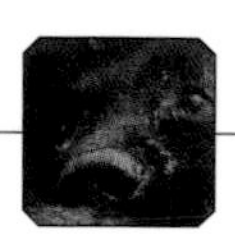

since they did it unconsciously. They knew large chunks of several children's books by heart: *Danny and the Dinosaur* and *Danielito y el dinosaurio, Stone Soup* and *Sopa de piedras, Horton Hears a Who!* and *¡Horton escucha a quién!*

Tonight they were doing English tongue-twisters from a new book that Valerie had given them. Erlinda read each one aloud slowly, and then the twins raced through it as fast as possible.

Erlinda said, "Okay, next one. 'Soldiers' shoulders shudder when shrill shells shriek.'"

Teresa began, "Soldiers' shoulders shudder when—what?—I forget what comes next," while Deanna shouted, "Shells don't shudder!"

Erlinda laughed and said, "Not a beach shell. A war shell."

Deanna yelled back, "That's stupid! Wars don't have shells!" while Teresa said worriedly, "What's 'shudder'?"

Erlinda shouted over the din, "Again! 'Soldiers' shoulders shudder when shrill shells—'"

Deanna interrupted. "Oh, yeah! Soldiers' shoulders shake when shrill—" and was herself interrupted by Teresa, who yelled, "No, not 'shake'—'shudder.' *¡Idiota!*"

From the kitchen, Valerie's voice said sharply, "Hey! Language!"

Erlinda collapsed helplessly on the floor, giggling. The twins danced around her, stage-whispering loudly. Soldiers' shoulders shake while shoppers shoot ships. Shells and shutters show shirts to shrimps. Seventy *soldados* sell shoes to *señores y señoras*.

Erlinda laughed so hard her stomach hurt.

It didn't take long for the new pups to begin showing clinical signs. Ceci had given Erlinda a list of what to expect: gastrointestinal disturbances, anorexia, behavior changes. But anticipating these signs in the abstract was quite different from actually cleaning bloody diarrhea and bloody

vomit off the cage floors, out of the water and food bowls, and off the puppies' faces, feet, and hind ends. The explosions got so frequent and so fierce that Erlinda began coming in an hour earlier every day to give the room an extra cleanup. She frequently found pups with dried feces and vomit clumped in their fur. At first, she tried to cut the clumps out. Soon, though, she began shaving the pups. It saved time in the long run.

The diarrhea and vomiting were ugly and smelly, but they were manageable. More distressing were the behavior changes, which got much worse during the second month of the experiment. A few formerly friendly pups became aggressive, growling and snapping at Erlinda or at one another when she had them out on the floor for cage cleaning and exercise. One little guy got so dangerous—barking and snapping violently, foam spraying from his mouth—that Erlinda decided she could no longer take him out of his cage. She felt bad about hosing down his cage with him in it, but she had no choice.

Most of the pups went the other way in their behavior. Some cowered in the corners of their cages, trying to hide, shrieking hysterically when Erlinda tried to pick them up for weighing. Others lethargically stared into the distance, looking at the fresh food she put in their bowls with indifference. She tried to tempt one with warm canned food—more aromatic and juicy than the dry puppy chow—but he showed no interest at all. She tried the canned food with another pup. Without getting up from his lying position, he sniffed it and licked once or twice. But eating seemed too difficult, and he gave up.

When Erlinda called Ceci to report which pups were suffering from dehydration or starvation and to ask if she could put them down, she was told no. Ceci said doing that would skew the data. She wanted the natural death dates recorded.

The husky black Newfie was the first to go. When Erlinda found him one morning, he was already cold. His shaved body was covered with bloody feces and vomit. He'd probably had a seizure before he died, thrashing and rolling around, spreading the mess.

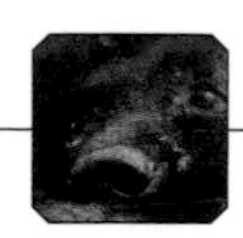

Erlinda didn't have to clean him up. It was a waste of time and therefore poor procedure. But she did. She washed him slowly and carefully before sliding him into a bag and putting him in the freezer. He'd be picked up for incineration on Thursday.

Somehow, Ceci found out that Erlinda had requested permission to switch maintenance responsibilities with Tony or Lollie for a couple of weeks. She needed a break from the dogs. But her request had been denied.

Ceci suggested that Erlinda accompany her on a visit to meet a child with lead poisoning. She said, "It's not fair for you to see only the depressing part of the experiment. Wouldn't you like to meet one of the people the experiment is designed to help? See the human face of the work?"

A good idea. Might help, couldn't hurt.

Ceci explained the situation to Erlinda. Mrs. Castillo, worried about her four-year-old son's speech delay, had taken him to the local pediatric clinic run by the university hospital. The pediatrician had found no structural defects in the child's vocal or auditory organs. His hearing tested okay, though not great. He tested positive for mild anemia. But the alarm had sounded when his blood test revealed a level of lead at 48 micrograms per deciliter. The pediatrician had reported the case to the health department, which had ordered a home inspection and family consultation. Ceci, who had gotten herself certified as a lead inspector for the sake of her research, had been assigned to the case.

Erlinda said, "Forty-eight what? I don't have any sense of what those numbers mean."

"Well, the trigger number is ten—ten micrograms of lead per deciliter. At ten or above, you've got lead poisoning."

"So this kid has a level of lead that's nearly five times the trigger amount? How could he accumulate so much in just four years?"

"Oh, he was probably born with plenty. If his mother had elevated lead levels while she was carrying him, the umbilicus would have funneled concentrated lead directly to his undeveloped brain and nervous system."

"So does the mother have elevated lead levels?"

"She doesn't show any clinical symptoms that I know of, and she hasn't been tested yet. But an adult can tolerate a lot more without impairment than a fetus can."

"How serious is this kid's speech delay?"

"Pretty serious. He's never made a sound."

"He doesn't speak at all? No sounds at all?"

"Nope. Nothing. *Nada. Nunca.*"

"Wow. Why did the mother wait so long to get him to a doctor?"

"I dunno. Her first child. Maybe she didn't realize anything was wrong. Or she thought he'd outgrow it, or she didn't have the money, or she was afraid. Or, or, or. You know."

"Yeah, I know. But it still pisses me off."

"Well, you can stop being pissed off. She understands now."

A child who had never uttered a single syllable. Erlinda tried to remember some famous quotation she'd heard about how language was what elevated humans above other animals. She thought of her nieces, Deanna and Teresa, so full of words.

Erlinda drove the hospital van slowly down Valencia while Ceci looked for house numbers. When Ceci said, "This must be it," Erlinda parked in front of the faded pink adobe house.

As they walked between the two scruffy mesquite trees flanking the entrance, Erlinda asked, "How old are these houses?"

"They might date back to the 1880s," answered Ceci. "A few still have their original saguaro-rib ceilings."

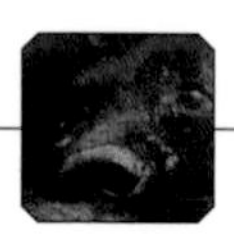

A young woman opened the door.

Ceci said, "Señora Castillo? I'm Dr. Ortiz from the university hospital. This is my colleague, Miss Tapia. We're here for the lead inspection. Would you like us to speak Spanish?"

The young woman said, "No, English is okay. Come in."

As Erlinda entered, she surreptitiously glanced at the ceiling: saguaro ribs. Too poor for new ceiling tiles.

After some brief pleasantries with Mrs. Castillo, Ceci took her clipboard and began the walk-through. While she did this, Erlinda sat in the living room and talked with Mrs. Castillo about the weather, family, and so on. Finally, Erlinda said, "What's your son's name? May I meet him?"

"Eduardo. Eddie. I'll get him."

Eddie was pretty small for a four-year-old. He sat on his mother's lap, sucking a finger, not looking at Erlinda. Not looking at anything, apparently.

Erlinda didn't want to ask him a question that needed to be answered orally, so she said, "Hi, Eddie. I'm Miss Tapia. How old are you?" He could just hold up the correct number of fingers.

Nothing.

Louder: "Eddie? *¿Cuantos años tienes?*"

Nothing.

But his hearing had tested okay. Did he ever respond to a human voice? Thunder? The smell of food cooking? Warm bathwater? Anything?

She asked.

"No. Nothing."

So this wasn't just a speech delay. This was serious brain damage.

Erlinda watched Mrs. Castillo stroke Eddie's hair away from his forehead. Watched her put her arms around him to keep him secure on her lap. Watched her kiss his cheek.

Watched Eddie do nothing. Watched his dull, changeless eyes staring at nothing. Staring at his nothing future.

Erlinda had come prepared to provide Mrs. Castillo with referrals

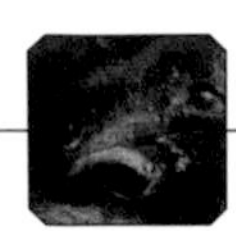

to the local Head Start program, to speech therapists, to private tutors. But she didn't mention the referrals. She looked down at the papers on her lap, pretending to read.

Just then, Ceci came into the living room carrying a ceramic bean pot. Every Chicano kitchen in the Southwest had a bean pot. Erlinda's mom had a plain brown one that she had brought with her when she left Cananea. But the pot in Ceci's hands was no ordinary pot like Mom's. It was a glorious thing, covered with flowers and leaves of green, red, yellow, and orange over a vivid black-and-white-checkerboard background. The rim of the pot and its lid were glazed a brilliant cobalt blue, as was the knob on the lid.

Seeing the pot, Mrs. Castillo smiled for the first time since Erlinda and Ceci had arrived. Erlinda felt a stab of anger and sadness. This woman's child didn't make her happy, but the stupid pot did.

Ceci asked, "Is this Talavera work?"

Mrs. Castillo smiled all through her answer. Yes, made in Puebla, her family's home. A wedding gift from her parents. Yes, she did use it to cook beans, at least twice a week. Beans and tortillas were pretty much all Eddie ate. He didn't like milk, fruit, or green vegetables. Ceci praised the pot's beauty and stepped into the kitchen to put it back where she had found it. As she returned, her eyes met Erlinda's for a second.

Suddenly, Erlinda knew what was coming—knew but didn't want to hear. Not after seeing Mrs. Castillo smile. She excused herself and went outside to wait for Ceci in the van. It wouldn't take Ceci long to tell Mrs. Castillo that she must never again cook anything in her beautiful, tainted pot.

As Ceci got into the van, Erlinda said, "How'd she take it?"

"She's pretty shaken, but she didn't protest. I told her that someone from the health department would have to take it away for sampling."

"Did you tell her that they'll have to destroy it?"

"No. The health department guy can tell her."

Erlinda started the van, pulled away, and drove silently for a while.

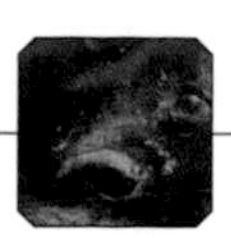

Ceci wrote down details of the inspection and interview while they were still fresh in her mind. After a few minutes, Erlinda asked, "So now what?"

Ceci continued to make notes as she talked. "Well, I'll write up the case and submit my report to the health department and the examining pediatrician. Then I'll add the case numbers to the database."

Erlinda said, "No, I mean—what will happen with Eddie?"

"Oh. I suppose the pediatrician will recommend that Mrs. Castillo start Eddie on intensive chelation therapy, probably with EDTA."

"What's that?"

"Ethylenediaminetetraacetic acid. It bonds with the lead in the bloodstream so it can be eliminated in urine."

"How is this stuff administered?"

"Intravenously. It's a hospital procedure. Each session takes about four hours."

"Each session? How many sessions will he need?"

"Well, considering his lead level, I'm guessing that it might be as much as a hundred sessions. Maybe twice a week for fifteen months or so."

"Man! That's a lot of needle time for such a little boy. And his mother will have to figure out some way to get him across town to the hospital twice a week. For over a year."

They were stopped at a light. Erlinda looked over at the clipboard on Ceci's lap and noticed that Ceci was no longer writing but doodling, filling in her zeros and eights with delicate cross-hatching. Ceci said, "There are buses."

"She'll have to take a lot of time off from work. She doesn't get paid if she doesn't work."

Ceci continued doodling.

"But after this treatment, he'll be okay? Do you think he'll ever speak?"

"Oh, I dunno. Depends on a lot of things."

"Like what?"

"Well, their house probably has so much lead that abatement might not be possible. The health department may order it condemned."

"So they'll have to move. What else?"

"Um. Let's see. His diet will have to change pretty dramatically. The lead from the cooking pot that's been leaching into his beans has made them taste sweet. That's probably why he doesn't like other kinds of food. His mother will have to get him to eat a wider variety of nutritious foods."

Erlinda was quiet for a minute. Beans were cheap. Fresh fruits and vegetables were expensive. Then she said, "Anything else?"

Ceci concentrated on her doodling. "Well, chelation therapy can have some pretty serious side effects. It often removes essential minerals as well as lead. Calcium, for instance. A low calcium level could lead to bone damage. And zinc. Zinc deficiency could lead to cancer."

Erlinda exploded. "Wait a minute! I thought you wanted me to see one of the people who would be helped by your experiment. How is Eddie being helped by all this?"

Ceci said irritably, "Linda, I didn't mean Eddie specifically. I'm hoping my research will help people like Eddie in the future. And maybe reduce the frequency with which Eddie's problem gets replicated in the population."

After a minute, Erlinda said, "Yeah, I hope so, too. But as far as Eddie's concerned, he's just up the creek, isn't he?"

Ceci shoved her clipboard into her bag and said, "Maybe. Oh, Linda, I'm sorry. I didn't intend to mislead you about Eddie's future. I know his situation is really sad."

Erlinda inhaled deeply and concentrated on driving. After a few minutes, Ceci said, "Oh, hey, here's that issue of *Scientific American* I was telling you about, the one on environmental pollution. Lots of good stuff about lead. Want to borrow it?"

"Sure. Thanks."

They drove the rest of the way to the hospital in silence.

Erlinda lay in the dark, her brain fixed on the cover of the magazine Ceci had handed her. Goya's *Saturn Devouring His Sons*. A raw image, rough, dark. Saturn, a crazy-eyed, lank-haired, red-faced giant, clutches a small naked body, his fingers biting deep into its back. The child's head and arms are already gone, presumably down the giant's black maw. The stumps of the child's neck and right shoulder run with gore. The giant's face expresses a bottomless hunger, a wolf in the stomach so ravenous it will never sleep.

Insatiable. Saturn. The planet that rules lead.

She thought of the leaded fumes that Leo inhaled every time he gassed up his beloved Impala. Or sat in traffic or used a drive-through window. That his wife and kids inhaled if they were riding with him.

The water that pumped through the old lead pipes in Mom's house. That she cooked beans in. That she drank. That seeped into her skin pores when she bathed.

The lead-based paint that coated the inside and outside of Mrs. Castillo's house. Flaking and chipping into invisible particles picked up on shoes and clothes, tracked through the house, floating and settling on cigarettes and dishes and glasses and silverware and food. On everything that went into Eddie's mouth.

The bare dirt around Erlinda's old duplex. Full of lead particles left over from its construction. From the welding, sanding, painting, plumbing, soldering, stripping, cutting, and grinding. Blown in on the ever-present dust through her swamp cooler, blown into her nostrils and mouth.

The lead-based home remedies that Tía Rita used: *greta, luiga, rueda*. Things she recommended for arthritis, infertility, upset stomach, menstrual cramps. For colic in babies.

The lead-sweetened candies that Leo's kids loved. Tamarind and coconut rolls. *Chapulines*, those crunchy grasshoppers toasted with garlic and lime. *Chaca-Chacas*.

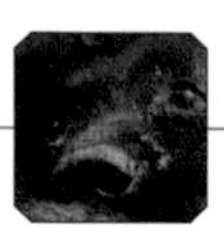

The lead in Valerie's extensive collection of herbs and spices. From crops contaminated by pesticides, exhaust emissions, metal particles from the grinding process, soil residue, drying over open fires. Chilis, cilantro, oregano, garlic, black pepper.

Erlinda's lead-based crimson lipstick. Worn for the first time at her *quinceañera* party six years ago and reapplied several times daily since then. A sentence she'd read in Ceci's magazine stuck in her head: "The average woman ingests six pounds of lipstick in her lifetime." Mom's raven hair dye, Ceci's black mascara.

The lead-based paint on the family crib, carefully stored in Mom's shed for when Erlinda had kids. The paint already chewed by three generations of children.

Infructuoso. Inservible, ocioso, vano, inútil.

Futile.

Erlinda usually enjoyed her drive to work. Leaving home before the roads clogged with morning rush-hour traffic, she focused on the silhouette of the mountains as she drove. That's how she had learned to navigate. The flattish undulations of the Rincons showed her when she was headed east. The fringy scalloped points of the Santa Ritas, south. The gentle humps of the Tucsons, west. And, as she drove north to work at sunrise, the sharp peaks and rock pillars of the Catalinas. She hated to drive in other cities because she got hopelessly lost without the mountains to guide her.

Today, though, she couldn't focus on the mountains. She drove robotically, turned inward, steeling herself against the moment when she'd have to face those lead-poisoned puppies again.

Why now? She'd been dealing with dogs as lab specimens for three years. She'd defended her job again and again to people who couldn't understand why she did it. The arthritis experiment, for instance. Each

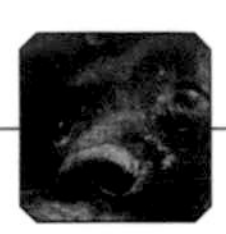

of the dogs in that room had its right hind leg pinned up, bent and useless, so the induced arthritis could freeze that leg in place. But nearly all of the dogs had adjusted well to functioning with three legs. Like foxy Zorro, her favorite, who had as much spirit and energy as any four-legged dog. He didn't even seem to notice his useless leg. And this experiment would really help people. The researcher, Dr. Guzman, had told Erlinda that medical science had made a lot of progress in controlling arthritis, that he actually expected they'd discover a cure within her lifetime. When Erlinda thought about being a part of that cure, she felt good.

But lead poisoning was different. The pups in Ceci's experiment hadn't—couldn't—adjust. They were miserable. And now, after learning about the pervasiveness of lead in the environment, Erlinda didn't believe that Ceci's experiment could possibly accomplish anything.

Consciously shifting focus, she forced herself to look at the mountains as she drove, at the patches of pink-gold morning sunlight dissolving the indigo shadows.

But a few minutes later, her mind was back with the pups. Misery and futility.

This morning, when she walked into the arthritis experiment room, she froze. Every cage had a "Do Not Feed" sticker on it.

Zorro. She forced herself to turn, to look at his cage. Like the other dogs, he ricocheted back and forth between his steel walls, yipping breathily in the manner of devocalized dogs, ecstatic to see her. Oblivious to the deadly orange sticker on his cage door.

Do not feed. The lab animals never got a last meal. They died empty. Less mess for the lab techs to clean up. The arthritis experiment was over. Brad and Dr. Guzman would kill the dogs tonight. Zorro would die tonight.

And she'd clean his empty cage tomorrow. All the empty cages. For a new batch of dogs. For a new experiment. For some researcher to use as a professional stepping-stone. To write papers on. To deliver lectures

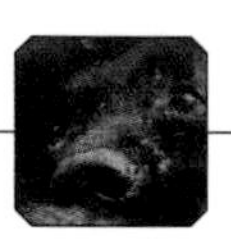

on. In the interest of science. For the benefit of humanity. While Erlinda hosed down the shitty cages and waited for the dogs to die.

She opened Zorro's cage door a few inches and stuck her hands in, grasping the dog's red ruff, scratching his neck with strong fingers. He shoved his wet black nose against the inside of her forearm, nuzzling and licking.

A moment of fantasy: Steal him! Get him out of the building before anyone else arrives! Put him in the car and drive away fast!

The cold wash of reality: A crime. The steel pin surgically attached to his leg, the ear tattoo, the severed vocal cords—clearly a lab specimen, readily identifiable, obviously stolen. She probably wouldn't even get him across the parking lot before being caught. She'd have a felony record, and Brad would kill Zorro right on time.

She gave the dog a final scratch, gently pushed him back inside his cage, and left the room.

Not thinking, moving automatically, she walked to the locker room. Took the name badge off her lab coat and dropped it into the wastebasket. Took off her lab coat and dropped it into the laundry bin. Exchanged her lab-owned rubber boots for her street shoes. Got her purse out of her locker. Walked to her supervisor's office. Wrote a note telling him to call Brad in for a double shift today. Telling him she wouldn't be back.

She stood outside the hospital at the top of the long flight of steps leading down to the parking lot. The steps glared bright white in the midmorning sun. She put on her sunglasses and began to walk down.

MOTHER LOVE

San Francisco, 1993

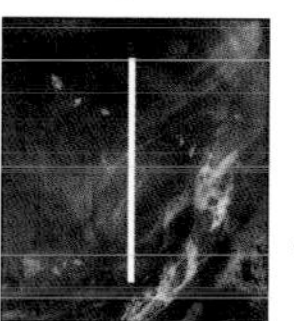

t wasn't called sexual grooming back then. And the shrunken head—the *tsantsa*—wasn't the usual expensive designer jacket or Hammacher Schlemmer über-toy.

Janey sat sideways across the upholstered wing chair, bare legs dangling over the arm, looking at photos of naked Amazon Basin people in *National Geographic*. She raised her eyebrows at her mother. "No way! Where did you get that?"

Denise handed her the wooden pedestal with the shrunken head on it. "Hey, aren't ten-year-old girls supposed to be reading Nancy Drew or something?" She laughed to show her approval that Janey was not reading Nancy Drew. "A private collector sent me some photos a couple of months ago and asked if I wanted to buy it. He'd gotten it illegally, of course, and couldn't sell it on the open market, so I said sure. Just a tiny lapse in my professional ethics." She smiled and winked at her daughter.

"So it's yours? Hey, are the eyeballs still in there?" Janey turned the pedestal, admiring the worried-looking forehead, the furry eyelashes, the snoutlike nose, the miniature ears.

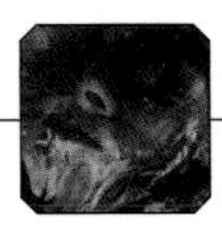

"No, the eyes are gone. The skull, eyes, and brain would have been tossed in the river right after this guy was murdered and decapitated. The head is hollow, like a bag. And no, it's not mine. It's yours."

Janey looked up in amazement. "Mine? Why?"

"Reminds me of your father. The strong, silent type."

Denise smiled again; Janey focused on the *tsantsa*. Then she set the pedestal on the coffee table and stood up to hug her mother. "Thanks! It's really neat."

Denise stroked her daughter's back. "Love you, baby." Even after coming home from teaching, she still smelled like the lemony stuff she used in the shower. Janey buried her face in her mother's wonderful hair—long, kinky, and dark blond, so fine it floated in the slightest breeze.

They nuzzled and burrowed into each other.

The *tsantsa* saw nothing.

Winter, late afternoon. Darkening, but the vampires aren't out yet.

Got my groceries and mail, safe at home now. Double-sided dead bolt clunks twice: once to let me in, once to keep them out.

First sight of home is my desk, supervised by the *tsantsa* on its pedestal. The head is fist-sized, with long black hair and charcoal-darkened skin. Wears a fluffy cap of orange and yellow toucan feathers and long tubular earrings of iridescent-green beetle wings. Most important, its eyelids are sewn shut, nostrils and ears plugged with pitch, lips laced together with cotton strings. The *tsantsa* guards my telephone and computer, dangerous conduits of communication with the world outside my studio apartment. Reminder: Loose lips sink ships. No loose lips here.

On the wall behind the *tsantsa*, my list:

- deep breathing exercises
- relaxation techniques

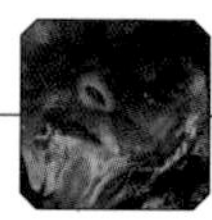

- hot bath
- music
- journal
- ~~incest survivor hotline~~

The last thing is crossed out because they always want to argue with me about semantics, about what is love and what isn't. I don't call them anymore.

The red light flashes on my phone. Even if I had been home, I wouldn't have picked up. Voice mail, caller ID, spam filters, firewalls—my armor.

No rush. (Door locked? Yes.) Spinach and carrots go into the fridge, Doc Martens exchanged for sheepskin scuffs. *Raag Charu-Keshi* on the CD player, volume low, bass high, tablas and sitar. Cold Sarajevsko Pivo popped open.

Finally, voice mail: "Janey."

My breath stops. Janey's gone. I am J.T. Janey is third person, past tense, passive voice.

"Janey. He was taken off chemo and the other IVs yesterday. No fluids, no nutrients. He'll go fast now. He wanted to have his hospice care at home, so I'm doing most of it myself. I know it's a long flight from San Francisco to Richmond, but please come. Come soon. It would mean so much." Her thin, tired voice.

To whom would it mean so much? Her, me, God? What would it mean to Dad? Anything?

I take the beer and sit in my only comfortable chair to watch the pallid sunset through the blinds, the graying view of Sausalito across the bay.

Haven't seen them for fifteen years. Placated Denise with letters and emails and excuses and promises. Apologized for my abrupt departure, for the hurt. Nudged our conversations into adult civility. Told her about my schoolwork and (later) my job, about interesting films or restaurants or books. Tossed in casual references to friends and coworkers

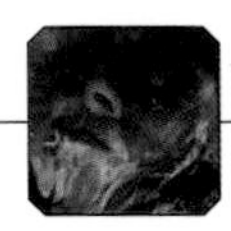

so she wouldn't worry that I was too isolated. Avoided talking about sex so she wouldn't worry about pregnancy or infection.

She stuck the odd check or book or music album/tape/CD (depending on the year) into packages containing long, confessional letters—letters all about her, ending with a couple of safe questions ("How's work?" "What's your weather like?") and "Much love from Denise and Mick." I call four times a year: his birthday, her birthday, Mother's Day, Father's Day. If he answers, he talks for two minutes and says, "Let me put your mother on." If she answers, she says, "He's not here right now."

Ten months ago, she added a P.S. at the bottom of my birthday card: "Mick's been diagnosed with prostate cancer, but the chemo/radiation should knock that out of his system soon. Wish us luck!"

I wished them luck and sent Dad a funny get-well card. Denise was noncommittal after that: chemo continues, trying a new drug, MRI scan shows no new tumors. Made it sound like a drag, not a death sentence. Maybe that's all she thought it was.

The pale sun is gone now, but I keep the lights off. The final notes of the raga fade away. Darkness. Silence.

Would a deathbed reconciliation be worth anything? I fantasize about his apologies, hers, the warm family embrace as I hold my father one final time. Maybe it would feel normal and right.

But I'd better take the *tsantsa* with me.

Janey's mother usually treated her like a small adult: no baby talk, no Santa Claus myth, no Mattel products. She was Denise, not Mom or Mother. Janey's father was Mick (except when Denise wasn't around, when he was Dad). Denise discussed all subjects freely in Janey's presence, pulling no punches with politics, religion, or sex. Janey had always known about the evils of the Vietnam War, muscle cars, and patriarchy. She felt superior to the other kids at school because there was no television in her house.

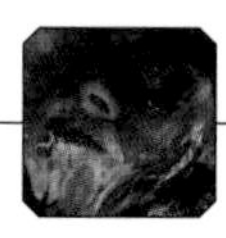

Denise was Janey's main caretaker. She had explained that this was not because she was the mother but because her work schedule was lighter and more flexible than Mick's. The university where Denise taught as an adjunct professor of anthropology was closer to home than the hospital where Mick worked nights as a nurse supervisor. (Denise walked; Mick commuted two hours daily.) As Denise fixed dinner for Janey, Mick kissed his wife and daughter good-bye, then shrugged on his jacket and fished for the car keys in his pocket.

Before Janey had started school, her time to be with Dad was afternoon, starting when she bounced him awake after her lunch. In her earliest memories, he's thirtyish with lots of bright brown hair and a bushy Fu Manchu mustache. She had loved to help him with little fix-it jobs around the house. He had given her a few miniature tools—real tools for small hands, not toys—so she could work with him: a bench vise, a hammer, and (best of all) a spirit level with that mysterious bubble inside.

Dad had great hands: warm and dry, slow and careful. He taught Janey by showing, not talking. They had poured a walkway in front of the house, and Janey pressed her small bare feet into the congealing concrete. Later, after the walk had set, rain collected in the impressions, and Janey squelched it out with her now-bigger feet. They had built a bat house and installed it under the roof overhang. No bats ever came. Dad thought they might need to be closer to the river.

After Janey had started school, she rarely saw Dad during the week. And his mandatory overtime, though Janey knew the family needed the money, often took a chunk out of his weekends.

At first, she missed working with him on the fix-it projects. Missed the clean smell of his soap and toothpaste and fresh cotton shirts. His raised eyebrows when she reported some particularly outrageous line of Denise's. His quietness, his lack of flash. Missed feeling peaceful and safe with him. After a while, though, he moved to the back of her mind. Denise sucked all of Janey's attention and energy.

Over the years, Denise's music became Janey's: Frank Zappa, Edgard

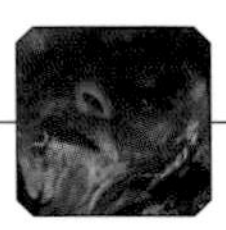

Varèse, Buddy Rich. Denise would play the fourth movement of Rimsky-Korsakov's *Scheherazade* suite over and over, laughing and cheering as Janey banged out the snare drum part on tables and countertops, practicing the rolls, fills, drags, and flams that Denise had taught her.

Denise also gave her collection of old posters to Janey. The kiddie art on Janey's bedroom walls was replaced by Art Nouveau-style ads for long-gone rock concerts, Pre-Raphaelite stunners by Rossetti and Burne-Jones, and even a valuable *Cosmic Runner* from 1968, signed by Peter Max. No longer did Janey wake up to powder blue and baby-girl pink; her morning eyes drank in acid green melting into vivid turquoise, overlaid by checkerboards of brilliant yellow and heart's-blood red.

The miniature carpentry tools slowly disappeared, replaced by some of Denise's anthropological artifacts, the ones she didn't keep at school. Janey's bookcase acquired a tall Karaja headdress of bright red macaw feathers, an extravagant Mayna pectoral heavily embroidered with pale cowrie shells, and a white Shipibo clay vessel decorated with geometric black mazes.

The prize, of course, was the *tsantsa*. Sitting on its pedestal on her dresser, it governed her room. It saw nothing, heard nothing, said nothing. It received, but never gave. Janey lay on her back in bed, watching it from across the room. Its presence was mysterious, spooky, but also strangely comforting. She never felt lonely.

While Dad worked nights, Denise experimented with exotic cooking, feeding Janey Ethiopian stew on sourdough flatbread or Afghani *qabili palau* with fried raisins and pistachios. Sometimes. Other times, Denise lay on the couch, tears trickling from the corners of her eyes. Janey made cheese sandwiches or heated canned chili and cajoled her mother into sitting up and eating a few bites. Then she'd put Denise to bed, do her homework, and lie awake in her room, watching the *tsantsa* until she got sleepy.

Meanwhile, Dad's hospital celebrated thirty years of community service with the completion of a hundred-million-dollar expansion: a new emergency department, heart center, ambulatory surgery center,

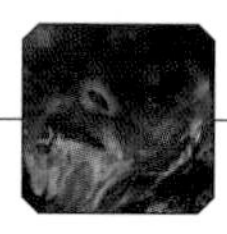

cancer clinic, and intraoperative MRI. Dad got promoted and stayed at work even more hours than before.

One night when Janey was thirteen, after a dinner of green corn tamales, Denise told her about "fibs," poems that follow the Fibonacci math sequence of 1, 1, 2, 3, 5, 8, with each number in the sequence dictating the number of syllables in each line. When Janey asked suspiciously if this was real poetry, Denise said, "Of course! This is syllabic poetry, which goes back long before Shakespeare. It's for intellectuals like us who don't need jangling rhymes. Come on, let's try." They wrote separately for a few minutes, then read their poems to each other. Janey had written:

hi
there
Mickdad
I hope you
like this fib poem
I wrote it just for you, for you

Denise's poem was:

my
own
baby
girl, daughter
of my flesh, I feel you
in, on, through, within . . . like my blood

"Oh, that's goopy!" Janey's face felt hot, so she got up from the table and went to get more mango juice. Denise stood up and caught her

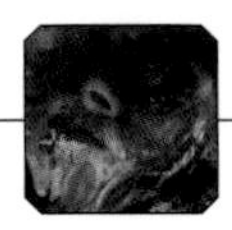

daughter, hugging her from behind and murmuring into her hair. Janey felt her breath coming hard for a minute or so before it slowed. Then she turned to face her mother, and the two of them embraced, rocking back and forth together.

After that night, Denise sometimes left fibs for Janey in secret places: her book bag, shoes, or jacket pockets. Some mornings Janey would see a scrap of white paper sticking out from under the base of the pedestal on which the *tsantsa* sat. And there would be a new fib, put there the previous night. Janey kept all Denise's fibs, stuffing the scraps of paper up inside the hollow head of the *tsantsa,* behind the sewn-closed eyes and mouth. When she was alone, she'd sometimes pull out the scraps, spread them on her bed, and read the poems all over again. They confused her, making her feel special but strange at the same time. Then she'd give up and stuff them back inside the *tsantsa* before replacing it on its pedestal.

At first, she tried to write some fibs for Dad, but she was never satisfied. They were babyish, not good enough. As soon as she finished one, she'd think it was fine. But a couple of days later, she'd see that it was stupid. After a while, she gave up trying. Then, after another while, she tried writing them again. She never gave any poems to Dad, though. They got stuffed up inside the *tsantsa* along with Denise's.

closed
eyes
see that
I love you
together we are
sphinxes with riddles but no words

Sometimes Denise told Janey bedtime stories. She'd say, "Once there was . . . ," Janey would supply a subject, and Denise would take it from there. But if Janey offered subjects that Denise thought were trite (a naughty girl, a family of three rabbits, an evil witch), her mother would

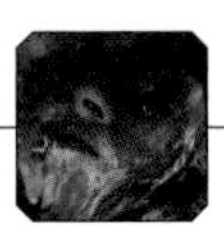

wrinkle her nose in derision and say, "Boring. I'm outta here. You'll have to do better than that tomorrow night." Then she'd sweep from Janey's bedside, leaving her daughter unkissed. But if Janey challenged her with an unusual subject—a psycho robot, a squashed tomato, a smelly turd—Denise would spin a wonderful story and reward Janey with tickles and kisses before the "Night-night, baby."

in
the
darkness
I wonder
what's in your brown head
do you ever think of me?

Janey's fourteenth year was utterly crappy. Couldn't get algebra at all. She had never felt stupid before. Or ugly, but now her face kept breaking out. Even her hair, grown long like her mother's, didn't help. Unlike Denise's hair, fine and floating, Janey's was lank and greasy. Sometimes Denise pushed Janey's hugs away, saying, "Ugh. You need a shower," or "You've got a real zit farm going there, kiddo." And a boy at school had killed himself, maybe on purpose, with an overdose of heroin. She hadn't known the boy very well—he was in a couple of her classes—but it was scary to think that someone she was used to seeing every day could just vanish from the universe.

Dad was quieter than ever. He no longer asked Janey to help him with his fix-it projects. Did he think she was too old for that stuff? He spent his scarce time at home reading or working on his computer. Did he think about work all the time? His mind seemed very far away.

One day Janey found a razor blade on the windowsill in the girls' bathroom at school. She didn't wonder why it was there—she knew several girls who cut themselves—but she did wonder what it would feel like. She'd heard that it was an instant rush, an immediate relaxation.

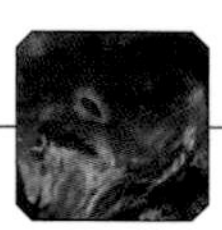

It was her lunch hour, so she had some time. She locked herself in the stall farthest from the door. Her first cuts were light and tentative, a few short slices on the insides of her upper arms. The pain and blood were interesting, novel, and she did seem to feel a flicker of relief. She pulled her jeans and panties down to her knees. Her next cut was firmer, more deliberate, a four-inch slice across her lower belly, just above where the pubic hair began. She sat on the toilet, legs apart, watching the blood trickle through the hair. Then she closed her eyes and leaned back against the cool tiled wall, her ugliness evaporating, the dirty black stuffing washing out of her body. Her breathing slowed and deepened. The air from the open window felt fresh on her face.

After the blood stopped, she reluctantly sat up and rough-cleaned her belly with damp toilet paper. There wasn't much she could do about the sticky matted pubic hair. She'd take a shower when she got home.

Had she thought about Denise's reaction when she picked up that razor? She couldn't remember.

That night, when Denise sat on the bed to say good night and saw the cuts on Janey's arms, she went ballistic. Yelling, "Any more?" she ripped open Janey's pajama top and yanked her pajama pants down to her knees, exposing Janey's whole body.

But when she saw the long, deep cut on the lower abdomen, her anger evaporated. She began to cry, loudly and convulsively, calling herself terrible names. As she wept on the bed, Janey comforted her, told her that of course it wasn't her fault, that it would never happen again, and so forth. Denise's sobbing quieted as Janey stroked her hair and kissed her neck and back. After a few minutes, Denise turned on her side and embraced her daughter. Janey was forgiven. Denise kissed the wounds to make them better, first the insides of the upper arms. Then the lower abdomen, just above the pubic hair.

in

the

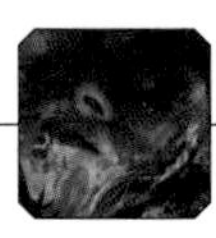

bedroom
the kiss cuts
like a feather edge
words are both blindfolds and razors

The cutting continued. As Janey gained finesse, she learned that even very small cuts could produce a great deal of blood from nipples, clitoris, and labia. She also learned that she could upset Denise even more by "excusing" the cutting with flippant one-liners: I had unprotected sex with Marilyn Manson. I disobeyed the sign and fed the bears. I turned on the shower and got sprayed by broken glass. I am a sacramental offering to Satan.

The cutting was a relief, but seeing Denise cry also made Janey feel good. Triumphant. And Denise always kissed the cuts—wherever they were—to make them better.

When Janey was sixteen, she began planning the separation. Her friend Russell helped her research colleges and universities. He requested that application forms and financial aid information be sent to his house. The school counselor suggested that Janey look into technical writing, a lucrative, expanding field that would fit her aptitudes. Meanwhile, Denise arranged for Janey's acceptance by the university where she taught so Janey could continue living at home. Mick said that whatever the two of them wanted was fine. Janey let it happen.

But she secretly decided on California State University East Bay. San Francisco was big enough and far enough away from Richmond to be safe. With Russell's forged parental signature, she was accepted to the program five months before her eighteenth birthday.

On that day, she was gone. She took some jeans and T-shirts, her leather jacket, a few books, and the *tsantsa* with all the fibs inside.

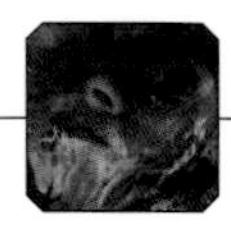

Everything else she left behind, even the valuable poster autographed by Peter Max.

The driver hands me my overnight bag and says, "Enjoy your stay in Richmond."

"Thanks."

The sidewalk in front of the house is now cracked and buckled from the roots of the tall dogwood. I remember helping Dad plant that tree as a sapling. I look for my footprints in the concrete. There they are.

Denise opens before I ring; she's been watching for me. She stands back to let me enter. Her wonderful hair is gone. She's cropped and gray, old and tired, purple smudges under her eyes. Her head looks like a skull. She falls on my neck. She seems very small. "Oh, baby. I'm so glad you're here. Come in."

I look over her shoulder toward the hospital bed in the middle of the living room floor. Something's on it, but it isn't Dad.

The smell. Sweet. Putrid. An inside-out smell, like my own menstrual blood on a scented pad. The smell sticks to the back of my throat.

Denise reads my face, says, "It's *fetor hepaticus*, the breath of the dying. His liver's failing." She leaves me standing, goes to his bedside. Picks up a sponge on a stick, a sponge-lollipop, sticks it in a glass of water, then into the open mouth on the bed. No teeth, a black hole. Down the rabbit hole. If I move, I'll fall in. "Janey, come and let him know you're here."

Can't look. Focus on the white sheet: small hills, valleys swell and fall, continually, slowly, obscenely. "What's that?" My voice sounds shrill, babyish.

"This electric air mattress prevents bedsores by constantly changing pressure points. Come over here and greet him. He probably won't respond, but he might hear you."

I can't. I focus on the plastic bag hanging on the side of the bed,

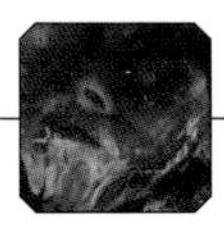

attached to the tube running underneath the blanket that's covering the belly, hips, and upper thighs. There's brown gel in the bag. Again, "What's that?" My voice is still shrill.

"Urine. He's on a catheter."

"Why is it so dark? Is there blood in it?"

"No, it's just concentrated. He stopped drinking a couple of days ago." She leaves him, comes to me, takes my hands. Hers are cold. I can't grip; she lets go. "Come on, now. He's been waiting for you. Let him know you're here." Her hand pushes my back, pushes me toward him.

Hair, mustache, eyebrows—all gone. Cheeks caved in. One eye stuck shut with hardened gray mucus; the other open a crack. "Can he see me?" Voice still babyish.

"Probably not. Dehydration impairs vision. But he might be able to hear you. You know, like when you hear the pilot's announcement on a plane? Sometimes you understand the words, but sometimes it's just noise? Go on."

There's nothing about Dad here. I don't see Dad, and I don't want this thing to be Dad. But I came to tell Dad that I love him, so I'll say it. "Dad." My voice is a whisper. "I'm here. I've come a long way to see you today."

No response.

She watches. "Louder. Tell him you love him."

Louder. Tell him you love him.

Louder, voice still too high: "I love you, Dad."

No response.

I sit next to the bed, hold his hand, mine sweating. Denise moves constantly, talks all the time—to me, not to him. He's not her husband any longer, just a thing to be tended to. She tells me what she's doing, what signs she's watching for.

She skims inside the mouth with the sponge-lollipop. Wipes the

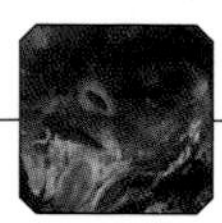

forehead with a damp cloth. Applies petroleum jelly to the corners of the mouth with a cotton swab. Applies lotion to the legs and feet. Straightens the blanket. Drops liquid morphine and diazepam under the tongue. Writes times and dosages on a yellow pad. Makes me take some of his tranquilizers. Closes the curtains at dusk, turns lights on low.

She keeps going. Keeps going.

There's nothing for me to do, nothing I can do. I sit on the couch and mechanically watch her mechanical movements. After a day of cross-country travel, with clock time everywhere, I've reached the end. If hours still existed, I would watch her for hours.

I watch her for hours.

After a while, she loses track of me and speaks to him. Sometimes I hear her tell him what she's doing and why: "Mick, I'm putting medicine under your tongue to help you relax. You don't have to swallow." Mostly, though, I can't hear what she says because her mouth is so close to his ear.

He never responds.

I think about my fantasy of a final family reconciliation. How naive.

Later, asleep on the couch, I miss his exit.

The morning is cold, rainy. They take Dad away. They take the hospital bed away. I shiver; Denise drapes the old afghan around my shoulders.

The living room windows are cracked open to air the room, to let in the cat-piss smell of the boxwood hedge in front of the house. Denise starts a fire in the old potbellied stove. Orange light begins to flicker through its translucent mica windows.

She brings me a mug of hot tea. Doesn't she remember? I've never liked tea. I say thanks and set the mug down.

She says, "Janey. Baby. Can you stay a day or two?"

I close my eyes and shake my head no. Janey is gone. I am J.T.

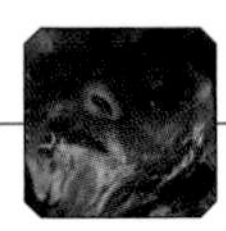

She turns her back to me and watches the rain trickling down the window. I'm supposed to go to her, hold her.

I don't.

My overnight bag is still sitting by the front door. I get out the *tsantsa*. I get out my folding blunt-ended travel scissors, the ones I'm allowed to take on the plane.

I snip the black stitches closing the eyelids and the white stitches closing the mouth. I dig the plugs of pitch from the nostrils and ears. The scraps of paper with the fibs on them show through the new openings in the head. The paper has turned brown.

Denise watches me, her face frozen.

I stick slivers of fatwood kindling into the neck opening and put the head on the grate.

It catches immediately. Flares shoot up, showers of sparks flitter, plumes of black smoke unfurl. A noise like cellophane crackling. The hair flames and hisses, a torch. The paper scraps blaze briefly, sending black bits spinning. Smell of burning charcoal, burning sulfur. The skin of the face relaxes, the lips and eyelids opening like petals, showing brilliance where darkness had been.

Only for a moment—then darkness again.

We watch the fire in silence. Her face shimmers, reflecting the orange light of the flames. She's crying, of course.

I'm not.

THE PUMP TWIN

Boston, 2000

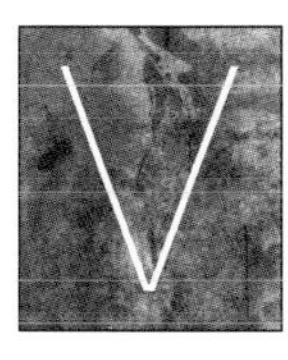oices above the surface.

Eight hours to remove the parasite's internal organs . . . amputate . . .

Who's speaking? Talking about what?

Nervous system disorganized . . . chaotic . . .

Circles of pink light. Spreading fast.

No paralysis in the autosite . . .

Bitter. Smell? Taste?

Four hours to suture . . .

Metal clangs. Water runs. Where?

Earlier separation . . . much simpler . . .

Murmuring, mumbling, laughing.

Twelve years old . . . quite late . . . psychological adjustment . . .

Tapping. Slapping?

Very close: "Daman. Are you awake? Can you wake up? Your father is here."

No moving. Closed. Cold cocoon. Sleep.

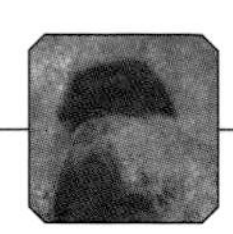

Later? Daddyji's voice: "Daman. Daman. Wake up now. Everything went fine. It's all over. All you have to do now is rest and recover."

What does it mean? Remembering. Today is the operation. Separation. Amputation. Something.

But Kalki's still here. I feel him, the weight of him, on my belly. He can't move either, but he's here.

I hear a whisper. It's me: "When will it happen?"

Laughter. Daddyji's voice: "It's already happened. It's over. It's done. You're fine."

Whisper: "But—Kalki? I feel him."

Daddyji's voice, harder now: "No. It's gone. You're normal now. Open your eyes and look."

White ceiling pocked with holes.

A cold hand slides under my neck, lifts my head. Blue walls, white sheets, silver metal things. Daddyji. My body, flat and bandaged.

I can't see Kalki, but of course he's there. Where else would he be?

We were born not one or two, but one and a half. Born with "twin reversed arterial perfusion." Our one heart was inside my body, making me the pump twin. His undeveloped lower torso and legs protruded from my abdomen, his vestigial head buried inside me. You can still see that ghostly head on the X-rays. His shoulders and arms never developed. When people asked me how it felt to have someone else's head inside me, I never knew how to answer. What does it feel like for you *not* to have a head inside your torso? "Normal"? There's your answer.

But Kalki wasn't dead—oh, no! I could always feel his life, our heart pumping blood through his body. I felt his temperature fluctuations, his toes stretching and flexing. He twitched constantly, even in his sleep. You know how you can use a ticking clock to simulate a mother's heartbeat, to

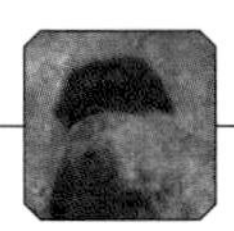

reassure an infant or a puppy? That's how his constant movements were to me—reassuring, comforting, like rocking in a cradle.

He smelled like life. Strange to say, I suppose, but the smell of life is piss and shit. (The dead produce neither.) He always wore a diaper, of course—he dribbled and dripped constantly—but his closeness to my nose meant that I always smelled him. I don't remember ever thinking that he smelled bad, I guess because the smell was always with me. It was just Kalki's smell, my brother's smell. Later, when I got older and more interested in our penises, I noticed that his sometimes got hard. I tried a few times to make him come, but that never happened. His smell was always babyish, never adolescent.

The doctors always called him the parasite. It annoyed me that they didn't use his name. After all, they called me Daman, not the autosite. Mamaji used his name and so did I, but no one else ever did.

Greg, my supervisor, looks worried. He shuffles through the papers on his desk. I know he's been arguing with some jackass in the Human Resources office. Greg's a good guy, he's on my side, but he's wearing out. He says, "Now, Daman, about this request you filed for reasonable accommodation. Why do you need this software? What's it called again? Yeah, this Dragon Naturally Speaking with PDF converter? Christ, Daman, it's nearly two thousand dollars!"

I feel sorry for him. It's been a bad year, budgets tight all around. He's had to cut back a lot, no training for anyone this year, no conferences. He even had to lay off our legal intern last week—our first intern from Harvard—and that really stung. She was great; we were all sorry to see her go.

I give it a shot in my brightest talking-to-the-boss voice: "Well, it'll help me create contracts, dictate briefs, and so on. It even does e-mail. Enormous legal vocabulary and . . . and it also formats legal citations." I'm

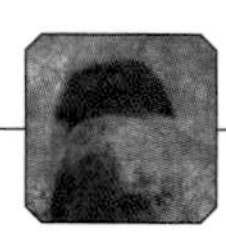

running out of bullshit, but I push out a few more words: "Let's see . . . builds templates . . . um, transcribes . . ."

Greg's worry lines deepen and his mouth tightens, so I stop talking. He sighs. "Yeah, I know all that. You attached the marketing blurb to your request." He leans forward and puts his forearms on his desk, hands clasped. "Daman, we've got to explain about *you*, not about the product. Why do you—*you* specifically—need this thing? We've got to have a documented disability. We need to prove that you can't do your job under the current conditions."

I scoot my chair back. My face feels warm. How do I explain this? "Well, it's just that I'm having a hard time getting close enough to my computer to use the keyboard."

Greg raises his eyebrows. "I don't understand. We bought you screen magnifier software last year. Have your eyes gotten worse?"

"No, no, that screen magnifier is great. It isn't that. It's not my . . . vision."

"So what is it, then?"

Silence. He stares at me. I know I should make eye contact, but I'm looking out the window.

Silence. He says, "Daman, I can't help you unless you help me."

I look back at him, but my eyes drop to his desk. "Well, it's my . . . arms, I guess. They aren't long enough to reach the keyboard when I'm sitting. I . . . uh, need the voice-activated software because I can't reach the keyboard."

His forehead softens. "Oh, I get it. Sounds like tendinitis or bursitis or something. You know, there are other solutions—cheaper ones." He smiles. "You could put your laptop on top of a filing cabinet and stand up to use it. Or we could get you a reclining desk chair."

"No . . . no. The chair's not the problem." I'm running out of excuses.

He thinks for a minute, then says, "Can you show me? Show me on my computer." He stands up and walks a few steps away from his desk.

Yeah, I can show him, but I'm starting to get a dragging feeling,

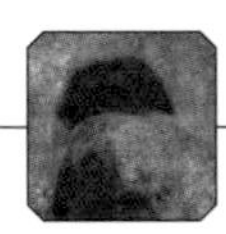

like this won't work, either. I sit down at his desk, face his computer, and adjust his chair so I'm comfortable.

"But you're—what?—a good twenty inches away from the desk. You can't get any closer?"

I look at his computer screen. There's nothing on it, just a bouncing tetrahedron, one of those default screen savers. He's a conscientious guy; he wouldn't leave sensitive documents up on the screen during an employee conference. I say, "It's hard to explain, Greg. I just can't. If I get any closer, I feel claustrophobic, like I'm suffocating."

I stand up, and we return to our chairs. Greg looks brighter. "A phobia, you say? Interesting. How about a therapist? We could probably get a referral today if we—"

Kalki kicks; I interrupt. "No. No therapist. This isn't something I can get rid of." Today, at least, I'm sure. As if I hadn't already thought about seeing a therapist a million times. As if a million times I hadn't already cursed Kalki for being born. Daddyji, for arranging the separation—or not arranging it much earlier, at our birth, before I knew Kalki. Mamaji, for giving birth to us, for teaching me to love my brother. Myself, for not being able to live without him, even years after he's gone.

Greg begins again, reassuring me—never say never, even the worst cases, blah, blah.

I interrupt again: "Greg, no. I *can't* get rid of it." Silence. "No therapist. I just can't."

We stare at each other for a minute. My face feels really hot now. His face clenches like a fist. I hate to do this to him. I hate to do this to myself. But Kalki . . .

Greg's eyes close for a second, then open. His mouth tightens. There's a long pause before he says, very evenly, "Well, Daman. I'm sorry. I don't think we can help you."

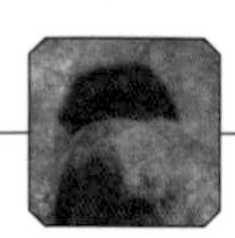

Mamaji was a devout Hindu. She wanted Kalki and me to have the appropriate ceremonies, but there were problems. During the Jatakarma, when new babies are welcomed into the world, Daddyji was supposed to drop ghee and honey onto our tongues. Then he was supposed to pierce our earlobes (so we'd have good memories) and whisper the name of God into our ears. But Kalki had neither tongue nor ears, so Daddyji was stymied. Also embarrassed, and he hated that.

But the ritual worked for me. I have a good memory. I remember Kalki all the time.

During the Namakarana, the naming ceremony, Daddyji named me Daman, "the controller," because I was the pump twin. Kalki's name, "destroyer of sins," was Mamaji's choice. Maybe Daddyji should have thought more about the meaning of Kalki's name before deciding on the operation.

Daddyji saw these traditional ceremonies as a waste of time and money. He didn't see Kalki as a person. Kalki was just an ugly thing sticking out of me, an excrescence like a wart or a mole. After we were born, Daddyji never made love to Mamaji again, so no more children. He just worked harder than ever, staying away from home as much as possible. Kalki and I were left to the care of Mamaji and the private tutors who came to our house to spare us the ordeal of going to school and being taunted by the other boys.

But Mamaji's guru said that God doesn't make mistakes. So Mamaji bathed and clothed Kalki until I got old enough to care for him. She trimmed his toenails. She put socks on his feet in cold weather. She never knew that he didn't like wearing socks—he'd kick and kick until I secretly removed them, then he'd settle down again. She made me promise that I'd always treat him like a brother, not like a wart.

When Mamaji died during our tenth year, Daddyji made some changes. He was determined that we would not continue to shame him.

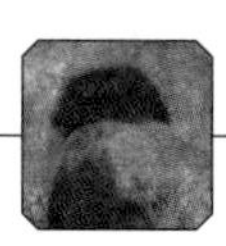

Many conjoined twins come from India and Italy, places that begin with I. Ironic, yes? Look at it: I is the most solitary letter in the alphabet. If Kalki and I had been born conjoined but equal, like Chang and Eng, we would have been an H. But we were born a Y. And now I'm just an I. Just I. But it always feels like we.

Anyway, some of those other conjoined twins earned money by exhibiting themselves. There were even some fakes, usually Anglo actors in brownface who attached rubber "twins" to their bodies. Daddyji has always had a healthy respect for money, but not money earned that way. He's an educated man. He didn't want ignorant fools throwing rocks at Kalki and me or (perhaps, in his mind, even worse) praying to us because they thought we were a manifestation of Vishnu. He had been outraged by the persistent approaches of an "entertainment entrepreneur" who wanted to display us in a circus. That was the last straw. His sons in a freak show! He sent us to live with our aunt in Boston, but he didn't intend for Kalki to stay long. He didn't want a pariah or a god or a monstrosity for a son; he wanted an engineer or a lawyer or a professor. One normal son, not two abnormal ones.

I did try to keep my promise to Mamaji. But Daddyji was stronger. He was our father, after all. I still wonder if there was any way I could have prevented the separation. We were only twelve. Kalki and I do the best we can with what we have left.

But every night, before sleep, we rewrite the past. We win the argument with Daddyji. Or kill him. Or run away from home. Sometimes we go with the freak-show guy. Sometimes we go to Tibet to become monks. Or to the beach at Orissa, where we hide out in the ruined Gopalpur temple. Make occasional appearances as Vishnu.

I protect Kalki. We stay together.

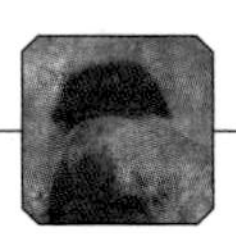

At first, Mona was okay with the bedroom rules. Maybe they seemed weird enough to be interesting, or maybe she thought they were exotic, like my dark body next to her light one.

But after a while she started to complain. "Too many don'ts, Daman. *Don't touch my stomach! Don't unbutton my shirt!* It's always got to be doggie style—I get tired of that. You never spoon me or hold me close. You've said your scar doesn't hurt, so what's the deal?"

She knows I had major abdominal surgery as a child. (I tell everyone it was Crohn's.) So I trot out the old "You know I don't want you to see my ugly scar. I'm really self-conscious about it in bed."

But it's not working this time. Her voice is impatient, not sympathetic. "Daman, I love you. I don't give a shit about your scar. Everybody has scars. I hate tippy-toeing around it in bed, always having to avoid it. I hate the way it keeps coming between us."

I laugh at the literalness of her objection, and, after a moment, she laughs with me.

She leans in to kiss me, leaving the usual space between our bodies, and says, "Okay, okay. How about something simpler: We'll do it in the dark. We'll leave the lights off. I'll keep my eyes closed. I'll wear a blindfold. We'll buy a whole wardrobe of blindfolds for me to wear in bed. How does that sound, me in a blindfold and nothing else? You get to pick a different one each night: the fluffy black marabou blindfold, the red leather blindfold with X's over the eyes, the black lace blindfold, the metallic-blue satin blindfold with the fringe, the—"

Her eyes are closed; she's pretending to be blindfolded. Kalki relaxes, I relax. I kiss her; she relaxes. I love kissing her. I haven't ever felt this close to anyone else—except Kalki, of course.

I've never told anyone about Kalki. But Mona and I are planning to get married. Shouldn't she know?

I try to anticipate her possible reactions to the knowledge, try to anticipate how her response might affect us. What if she got interested

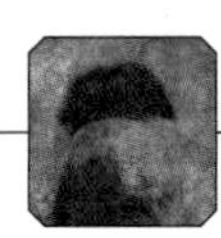

in him, wanted to know more, welcomed him to the family, treated him like a brother? Or like another husband? What if she just blew him off, thinking (like Daddyji) that he was a wart? Or if she laughed at his fantasies—his and mine—of running away together?

I don't like any of the possible reactions I can imagine her having. I need to think carefully about exposing him.

Now I'm annoyed. She's changing the rules after the game's begun. She's known from the beginning that I don't drive, that I'm not going to drive. One of our reasons for staying in Boston instead of moving to the suburbs was the public transportation system. Anyway, a lot of people don't drive here. Parking spaces are rare and expensive. Driving during rush hour is hair-raising and blood-pressure-raising. Auto insurance premiums are sky-high. Auto theft is a recreational sport. So I'm definitely not alone in refusing to drive.

Mona and I discussed all this before we got married, and she was fine with it. When we wanted to get out of town on a weekend, she drove. She liked having her own car, didn't mind maintaining and garaging it.

But now: "Daman, I'll need you to drive me to the doctor during the last trimester. I probably won't be able to get my baby belly behind the wheel. And of course you'll have to drive me to the hospital for the birth."

"No, I won't. We'll call a taxi. Plenty of pregnant women get to the hospital that way. I've even heard of women who drove themselves to the hospital while they were in labor."

She stares at me like I'm crazy. Then she shakes her head like she's shaking my words out of it. Her face and voice get hard (like Daddyji's). "Daman, please try to focus on the big picture, not on a specific example. There will be errands that need to be done by car, not by subway or bus. When I've got the baby, I won't be able to do them."

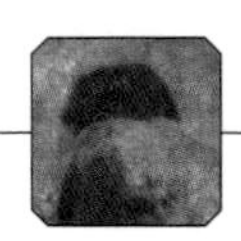

"So we'll hire a nanny with a car. It won't be a problem. I can get some referrals today from Jack. He and Melissa have used driving nannies for all their kids."

"Daman, stop it! You keep offering solutions to every problem except the one I'm talking about. You have to learn to drive!"

Kalki stiffens, his toes curling with apprehension. He hates being compressed; the steering wheel would make him feel like a prisoner. I say, "I've got to go. We'll talk about this later."

"Right. As usual." The sarcasm is automatic, not heartfelt. She looks tired and distracted. I don't kiss her good-bye, but she doesn't look like she misses it.

I don't, either.

"Daman, would you please take him for a minute? I need to duck into this rest room."

I take Jason, bending his legs up in front of him so they don't hang down onto my stomach. He's ten months old now. He's not really heavy for his age—only about twenty pounds—but he's definitely going to be tall. Already he's over thirty inches long and growing fast. I wish we'd brought the stroller inside the mall with us, but Mona said we'd be just a few minutes.

At first, I couldn't get enough of holding Jason. It was as if Kalki had returned to me. His toes spread out like a fan. The constant motion, twitching and fluttering, even in sleep. The smell of his dirty diapers—it was almost like being boys again together, back home, with Mamaji still there. Mona was amazed that I never complained about diaper-changing, that I was happy to do it all. The feeding was a different matter—Kalki hadn't needed that. But as soon as Mona finished feeding Jason, I wanted him back.

It came to an end one night when I was changing Jason on our bed. I was exploring his body, comparing him to Kalki, comparing his diaper

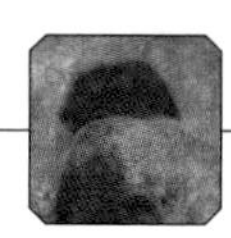

smells to Kalki's. I didn't know Mona had come into the room and was watching us until she said, "Uh . . . Daman, what are you doing?"

I jumped when she spoke, and my answer was louder than it should have been. "Nothing! Just changing him!" I fastened the diaper roughly, startling Jason and making him cry. She picked him up off the bed and gave me a strange look. I don't know what she thought I had been doing. She didn't say anything, just stared at me for a minute before taking the baby away.

Since then, she's always been the one to change him.

And now that he's older, he doesn't want me to hold him close all the time. He doesn't like me to keep his legs bent. He wants to dangle them, to stretch them out. But I don't want his feet kicking my stomach. That's Kalki's space. I won't be able to hold him much longer. I'll need to make sure that we always have the stroller with us.

Jason is really squirming now. I sit down on one of the wooden benches that surround the palm trees inside the mall, and set him on my thighs. He stands up and lunges to embrace my neck with his arms, pushing one foot hard into my solar plexus. I feel Kalki gasp with pain, and quickly thrust Jason away, holding him at arm's length on my knees. When Mona returns, he's crying. Again, she says nothing as she takes him from me. She and I talk less and less these days.

As far back as I can remember, I thought I could understand Kalki. I had this idea that when he straightened his left knee and stretched apart his left toes as if opening a fan, it meant he was cold and wanted to be covered up. And when he straightened his right knee and stretched out his right toes, he was too hot and wanted to be uncovered. Whether I was reading his signals correctly—whether these were really signals at all—I responded as I thought he wished, covering or uncovering him. Then his body would relax, and his legs calm down. I remember wondering if he

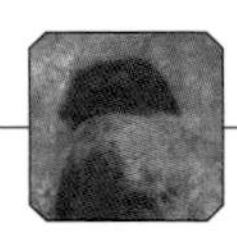

would get too hot when the cats slept in bed with us during our first winter in Boston.

As boys in India, we had known only feral street cats, teeming with scabs and fleas, that spent their lives scrounging for a bare subsistence, fighting to the death over the rotting fish eyes discarded in the city's household garbage, accompanying their rape-matings with bloodcurdling yowls, and spitting ferociously at any human who dared to approach them. So when Bua Shanti, our father's sister in Boston, introduced us to her indoor tribe of cats and kittens, we were initially fearful and even a bit disgusted. Many of our neighbors in Bangalore thought cats were vermin, no better than rats. But our aunt's gentle animals were so different from the feral cats that we soon lost our fear.

Kalki especially liked it when some of the kittens slept in our bed during the cold nights of that first winter in Boston. They burrowed under the blankets to nestle against us, and he rubbed his feet on their dry, woolly fur. He never kicked or showed any impatience with them. I know he couldn't hear them purring and chirping, but he always seemed to relax into sleep when they made these quiet noises.

His favorite kittens were Bali and Punit, who were often in our bed. They licked each other (sometimes pretty roughly), wrestled, kicked against each other's bellies, and bit each other on the back of the neck. Then they slept, curled up together in a ball with their heads, tails, and feet tucked inside.

At the time, I thought I was afraid that the kittens' thornlike claws might hurt Kalki. But maybe I was just jealous of his attention to them. The following spring, when Kalki and I were twelve years old, I began shutting the cats and kittens out of our room at night. I don't know if Kalki missed them.

That first year in Boston, Daddyji had arranged for us to settle in with our aunt, then have the surgery and recover from it before beginning school in our new life—or, rather, in my new life. He wanted me to have a fresh start.

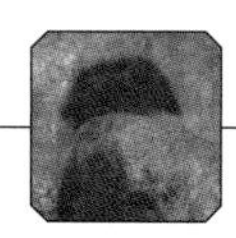

But I was lonely. Daddyji would continue to live in India, although he promised to be with us for the operation. I would probably never see my tutors or Mamaji's guru again. And Mamaji was dead. All I had left was my brother.

I didn't really understand what was coming. Daddyji had explained the surgery to me, of course, and I nodded my agreement, as he expected. But how could I imagine life without Kalki? If you can feel, smell, and love someone, how is it possible for that person not to exist?

Of course, Daddyji doesn't understand my self-imposed isolation. For a long time, his letters, calls, emails, and videos have been full of urgent paternal advice on doing my duty, living up to my responsibilities, and so on. He hasn't been harsh or judgmental—well, no more than usual. I think he really has tried to understand why I've given up on my family and my career.

But his urgency is lessening. When I made my usual Sunday call yesterday, his second wife spoke to me for a few minutes before putting him on the phone. "Daman, you know your father would never complain about his health." (Right; he'd see that as a sign of weakness.) "But he's having some real problems now with his high blood pressure and diabetes." (Ironic—he always joked that his big belly was a sign of prosperity.) "I know you were counting on us flying out to see you this year as usual, but I suspect his traveling days are over. You know you have a standing invitation to visit us anytime, for any length of time. And if you wanted to return to India to live" (she means now that my career and marriage have failed) "our house is quite large enough to give you all the privacy and space you need. Would you consider coming to us? If not to live, at least to visit? Soon? It might be the last time you see him, Daman."

My voice sounds sympathetic, reassuring. "Of course, Radha. I understand completely. I'll see what I can arrange." She knows perfectly

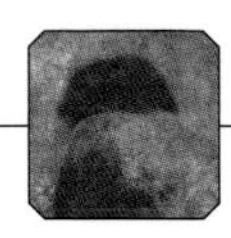

well this isn't going to happen, although she'll never understand why. Airplane travel is agonizing for Kalki, just like car travel. The travel time from Boston to Bangalore by air might be over twenty hours. And once we were there, we'd have to endure the same daily irritation of making excuses for what others perceive as our—my eccentric behavior.

Kalki and I are happy at home.

Her voice is subdued. "Okay, Daman. Here's your father now."

His voice sounds old, with an irritating whiny undertone that it didn't used to have. "Daman, I heard what she told you, and it's all bullshit! I plan to be around forever." He laughs, then coughs. "But if it takes a lie to get you out here, all right: I'm on the way out. That's what they think, Radha and your brothers." (Half brothers—I have only one real brother.) "They all think I'm going to go soon, but at least I won't die alone."

I smile. Neither will I.

BOY OF BONE

Philadelphia, 2006

r. Weisman stands at the lectern at the front of the crowded lecture hall. Many of the listeners lean forward, fascinated. They are physicians and medical students, and he is speaking their language. As the guest of honor, I sit in the front row to watch the projection of the black-and-white slides on the screen behind the doctor.

His language is not mine. "In early childhood the only abnormalities noted were bilateral hallux valgus and a fibrous fusion of the interphalangeal joint of the right thumb." On the screen is a skinny, smiling, big-eared boy of five years. He's wearing shorts and cropped hair, ready for summer. But instead of sandals or sneakers, he wears socks and clunky orthopedic shoes so you can't see his big toes angled inward, crossing over the tops of the second toes.

"In 1951, a fracture of the left femur precipitated the extraskeletal bone formation that continued for the next twenty-three years. Biannual surgeries removed the ossified tumor masses that occurred at trauma sites. Traction sessions, diethylstilbestrol therapy, vitamin E therapy, and back braces were used in attempts to slow the progression of the disease."

I think about Peter on that cool November afternoon, a few months after this photo was taken, when he and I were supposed to be

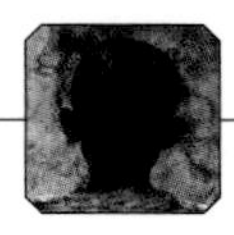

raking leaves in our backyard. Before we began, I made a line with my rake through the thick crust of fallen leaves, dividing the yard exactly in half and telling Peter to rake over there while I raked over here. I wanted him to do his fair share of the work, not get away with less because he was younger and smaller. I was ten years older than he and resentful that he was so often my responsibility. Our father was away from home most of the time, and our mother was frequently depressed, often spending whole days in bed sleeping or reading. So I was the one who usually took care of Peter. I intentionally raked slowly so as not to finish before he did.

Peter collected his leaves into many small, ragged piles, wielding the long rake awkwardly with his short arms and little hands. I demonstrated my superiority by raking my leaves into one grand mountain. When my leaves were piled, I ran toward the mountain, launched myself into the air, arced through space, and crashed softly into the crackling leaf-texture and intoxicating moldy leaf-smell. Envying my triumph, Peter ran toward my mountain and tried to match my jump, but he belly-flopped, feet still earthbound.

"Wait," I said. "I'll help you." I emerged from my leaf-burrow, grabbed Peter under the arms, and swung him toward the mountain peak. That was his final moment of joy, flying through the crisp autumn air, arms akimbo, laughing as he flew. That was the last time he ever laughed.

Our family doctor was puzzled by the fracture of Peter's left femur. I had searched the leaf pile but discovered nothing—no rock, no tool, no brick—that could have impacted the small leg with force enough to break it. Peter was hospitalized with traction on the broken leg. During the month he was in the hospital, he received no visits from his family. Our father was too tired when he got off work, our mother was too distraught, and I was too young—only fifteen, and hospital rules prohibited visitors under sixteen. That entire month I sat at home, suffused with guilt. This

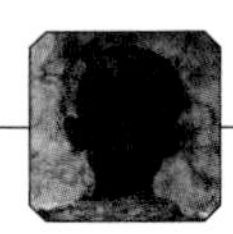

was all my fault. I should have been watching out for Peter, but instead I had broken his leg.

When Peter returned home just before Christmas, there was a bulge the size of a tennis ball on the front of his left thigh. This bulge grew quickly and was soon followed by a second bulge, on the inside of the same thigh. We learned that the bulges were bone, new bone forming on top of old. Peter's muscles were slowly transforming into bone. Later, we learned that his tendons and ligaments were also transforming into bone. He was growing a second skeleton over the first one.

Dr. Weisman's voice continues: "The initial diagnosis of myositis ossificans progressiva was changed to fibrodysplasia ossificans progressiva, called FOP, because it was discovered that the bone formation replaced not just muscles but also tendons, ligaments, and other connective tissues. Any minor trauma, such as a medical injection or a minor bump, could precipitate a new bone formation. Each formation began as a soft-tissue swelling that changed into bone in a process known as heterotopic ossification."

He changes the slide. The boy on the screen is now about fourteen years old. Unlike the five-year-old in the summer shorts, this one is wearing no clothes at all, just a medical G-string tied at the hips. He stands heavily on his straight left leg, right leg bent at the knee and slightly forward. The upper body and neck are flexed to the right about thirty degrees, the pelvis flexed forward about fifteen degrees. The boy holds his shoulders forward, hands together in front of his right thigh. His head leans right and down, eyes on the floor. He looks extremely uncomfortable. Unlike the little boy in the previous slide, this older boy is not smiling. This boy hasn't smiled in years. Neither has his sister.

By this time, Peter's spine had fused into a solid mass. Bridges of bone had formed to connect each vertebra to its neighbor. The fusion was

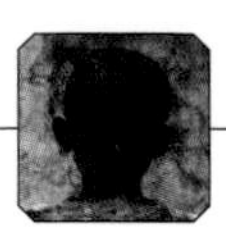

complete from tailbone to skull. Also, the muscles of his upper back had ossified, so he couldn't inflate his chest while breathing. Bone had also begun to form in the joints of the left knee and hip, the left elbow and wrist, and both sides of the neck. His jaw was beginning to freeze shut.

Dr. Weisman: "By the age of eighteen, Peter could no longer walk or speak. His teeth decayed but were inaccessible for treatment. He could still control his lips, so he was fed through a straw. The only other parts of his body that he could move were his right forearm and right foot."

Although I had graduated from high school ten years earlier, I hadn't gone to college or moved out to begin life on my own. I still lived at home to care for Peter. My father had left us, finding our domestic situation intolerable. We received the occasional postcard or check from him for a few years, but then nothing ever again. My mother had conceded Peter's care to me from the very beginning of his illness, she and I silently colluding on this decision. Not only was I younger and stronger than she, I insisted on doing it. Every day I fed, bathed, shaved, clothed, and unclothed him. I changed his diapers, filed his fingernails and toenails, adjusted the tension of his traction, and salved his bedsores. I administered his synthetic estrogens and vitamin E. I turned his television on in the morning and off at night, changing the channel throughout the day so he could listen to his favorite programs.

I did all this because it had to be done, and I was the only one available to do it. We couldn't afford a private nurse, and I refused to allow Peter to be institutionalized. But I also felt that I deserved to be punished by his pain, which was constant and excruciating. Every one of his movements and every one of his breaths was accompanied by pain—piercing, wrenching, stabbing, grinding pain. Every time I touched him, he moaned.

Our family physician, Dr. Emerson, had prescribed Demerol to control Peter's pain and had taught me to administer it intravenously. I did this twice a day or more, knowing that the needle's puncture could precipitate new bone formation. The relief of Peter's pain also threatened the worsening of his condition. This knowledge was part of my punishment.

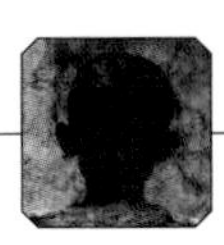

The Demerol reduced the pain, but it did nothing for the nightmares. Before his jaw had frozen shut, Peter had told me about them: every night, without respite, he dreamed of being trapped in a burning building, in a dungeon with knife-blades protruding from every surface, in a cell whose walls closed inexorably in on him. He had screamed every night for years. My mother had moved her bed into the dining room, as far away from him as possible. I slept on a small bed in his room. When he screamed, I spoke to him, sang to him, gave him another injection. I didn't dare touch him for fear of inflicting pain. When his jaw froze shut, the screams became quieter but more eerie, closed-mouth sounds like the expiring cries of a small mammal.

One day Dr. Emerson brought along another doctor and introduced her to me. "Margaret, this is Dr. Halate. She'll be taking over Peter's case while I'm on sabbatical next year. Before I leave her in charge, I want her to see how you and I do the weekly examinations."

I shook hands with the new doctor, wondering. She was not like anyone I had ever seen. Women doctors were unusual then, much more so than now, but Dr. Halate was unusual for other reasons, too. Short, round, and brown, she seemed solid and dense, like a rock. Her straight black hair was cut into a practical bowl shape, and her black eyes seemed expressionless as they glanced briefly at me. I later learned to read those eyes better.

The three of us went into Peter's room for the weekly examination, and I turned off the television. But when Dr. Emerson turned to Dr. Halate and began explaining Peter's history to her, she did a strange thing: Instead of watching Dr. Emerson's eyes as he spoke or looking at Peter lying in bed, she cast her eyes down to the floor. She didn't nod, blink, or fidget with her fingers. She just listened. She was a statue, like Peter. I watched Peter watching her. I expected him to become tense with the stranger in the room, but he didn't. Instead, the tension in his forehead and under his eyes and in his right hand appeared to evaporate.

The two doctors visited Peter together for the next several weeks. Because I was responsible for Peter's home care, I stayed in the room to

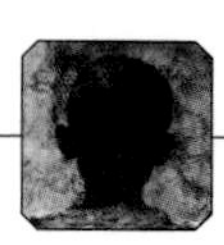

help with the examinations. While Dr. Emerson palpated Peter to discern any new soft-tissue tumors or formations of bone, Dr. Halate stood apart, not watching the examination, but listening. It was as though she could hear Dr. Emerson's fingers moving over Peter's painful flesh.

The week after Dr. Emerson left for his sabbatical, Dr. Halate arrived alone. She asked if I would assist her as I had assisted Dr. Emerson, and I said, "Of course." But when I turned off the television and began to undress Peter as usual, she stopped me. "No need," she said. "Just sit quietly and listen." I remember she didn't say "watch." So I sat in the chair on the left side of Peter's bed.

On the right side of the bed, Dr. Halate surprised me by sitting on the floor. Because the bed was low to allow me access to Peter, her head was level with his. Peter seemed surprised, too. It had been a very long time since another face had been so close to his. I hadn't kissed him in years, afraid of hurting him or causing new bone formation.

Dr. Halate sat in silence, legs crossed, back to the wall, eyes closed. I also listened. I could hear Peter's stertorous breathing, which had gotten increasingly louder during the time that the muscles of his upper chest and back were turning to bone, preventing his rib cage from expanding when he breathed. I could also hear my own breath, but not Dr. Halate's. She didn't speak, and neither did I. Peter's breathing grew quieter after a few minutes, but I was unnerved by the silence in the room. The only time I turned off the television was when Peter's visitors were talking, but this one wasn't talking.

Then Dr. Halate put something into Peter's right hand, and his fingers closed around it. She stood and said to me, "I have something better for the pain. Come with me into the bathroom so I can show you what to do."

Later that evening, after I had injected Peter and he was asleep, I removed the new object from his curled fingers. In the dark I couldn't tell what it was, so I took it into the bathroom and set it on the counter to look at it in the light.

It was a bear carved of stone. The bear stood upright about three inches high, round-bottomed, hump-backed, and paunch-bellied. He stood on one back foot, the other raised as though in dance. His front paws held a fish up to his long snout, and the expression in his red stone eyes was undeniably celebratory. Whoever had carved this bear had captured the soul of the living animal.

I picked up the bear and examined him more closely under the light. He was carved from a black stone vividly patterned with white starbursts that exploded randomly through the darkness. The fish was carved of a different substance, something softer, colored with iridescent streaks of blue and green and pink against whitish, watery pools that interrupted the streaks at intervals. The fish's bright iridescence against the bear's darkness made a complete thing, an entirety. I had never seen anything so wonderful.

Before I went to bed, I returned to Peter's room and set the bear on a bedside table, relieved to hear his quiet breathing in the dark.

When Dr. Halate arrived for her visit the following week, I told her how much Peter liked the bear and how beautiful it was. She surprised me by saying, "No, not beautiful. I wouldn't give him a beautiful thing." She looked around the living room and said, "There. That lamp is beautiful." She nodded at a table lamp that my mother had bought at the same time she had bought everything else in the room. She had gone to one of those furniture warehouses where everything is always on sale and had bought the first living room display she saw: mass-produced nondescript furniture with a shiny plastic finish on the wood, a machine-made imitation Persian rug in garish colors, and a trite landscape machine-printed and framed in gold plastic. And the lamps, a matched set: a table lamp, an accent lamp, and a floor lamp, all with the same gold-sprayed molded plastic bases and blowsy red shades that bathed the room in blood when the lamps were turned on at night.

I was incredulous. "You think that lamp is beautiful? What's beautiful about it?"

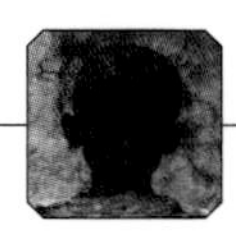

Dr. Halate considered the lamp before saying, "It's all the same thing. No surprises. If you turn it around, it will look just the same on the back as it does on the front. It just sits there. It never goes anywhere."

I didn't know how to respond to this, so I said, "And the stone bear is not beautiful?"

"No. A beautiful thing has no power. Peter needs a powerful thing, a dangerous thing."

"Oh. Well, he certainly loves that bear. It must be quite valuable. May I pay you for it?"

"No. Blessings are given, not sold." She turned and left the room to go see Peter, leaving me to contemplate my mother's beautiful lamp.

That night, after Peter was asleep, I took the bear into the bathroom and looked at him again under the light. I noticed things I hadn't noticed before. The edges of the bear's wedge-shaped tail, carved from its rump in low relief, were smooth, maybe worn down by fingers and palms over the years as they stroked and cupped the bear just as Peter's did now. I wondered how old the bear was. The bottom of the raised rear foot had a tiny chip on one side where the carver had made a mistake. I thought about the carver: Man or woman? Man, I decided. Old or young? Middle-aged. What had he thought when he misjudged and let his knife slip? He thought, "I need to quit for now and go eat something." Then, the next day, he looked at the chipped foot and thought, "It's not too bad. I'll continue."

Our mother, I think, suspected that Dr. Halate and I had made some change in Peter's treatment, but she asked no questions. Peter seemed better, quieter, less distressed, so she was content. When he was awake, he liked to hold his stone bear, moving his still-flexible right fingers in infinitesimal increments, feeling the cool stone gradually warming in his hand, feeling the smooth roundedness of the shape. Still able to move his right elbow and forearm, he sometimes brought the bear in line with

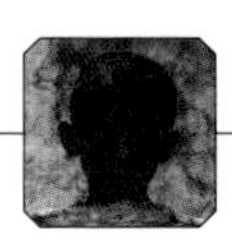

his eyes so he could see it turning in his fingers. He fussed less during the day, and at night, instead of moaning in protest at my approach with the syringe, he closed his eyes and relaxed, welcoming me. That was my signal to remove the bear from his fingers and set it on his night table until the next day. Because I slept in his room every night, I noticed when his nightmare screams began to lessen. Eventually they stopped almost entirely, and I had to get up much less frequently during the night.

Over the next few months, there were no painful weekly examinations with Peter being turned on his back and stomach, no traction, no sessions with the head halter or the back brace. In the beginning of Dr. Halate's time, I was worried that new bone would be growing unobserved, so I secretly palpated Peter once in a while as Dr. Emerson had taught me to. I never found any new growths, however, and since Dr. Halate didn't seem to think the hands-on examination was necessary anymore, I eventually stopped doing it. Every week she sat on the floor listening to Peter's breathing, then accompanied me into the bathroom to check and replenish Peter's supply of needles, syringes, and morphine.

Dr. Halate's new routine brought some peace to Peter and to me for a few months, but the three of us realized that the end would come soon. New strata of bone would continue to layer onto his rib cage, compressing his lungs and heart, causing slow suffocation. Once, as she was leaving our house for the day, she said, "Has Peter spoken to you of the end?" I said yes. I knew that he feared suffocation even more than paralysis or pain.

Other than this one oblique exchange, Dr. Halate and I never discussed my giving Peter an overdose. I knew, and she knew I knew, that the time would come when I would inject Peter with his week's supply of morphine all at once. I also knew, and she knew that I knew, that she would list cardiac failure as Peter's cause of death. I did ask her if she wanted Peter's stone bear back after his death, and she said no. She said it belonged to Peter whether he was alive or dead.

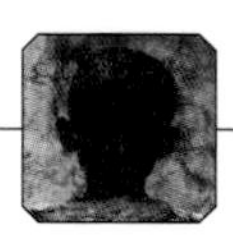

After Peter's death, I began sleeping twelve, thirteen, fourteen hours a day—my first solid sleep in twenty-three years. It was not a good sleep, though, not restorative. In a way, it was as though I had taken Peter's place. My body ached all the time; I couldn't speak; I rarely moved from my bed, which was still in Peter's room. My mother largely ignored me, believing me a malingerer, but every once in a while she'd make an appearance to give me a pep talk. She knew what real illness looked like (like Peter), and she couldn't see that anything was wrong with me. I should pull myself together. Now that Peter didn't need me, I should be helping her more. She was the one who ought to get some rest. She was the one who should be in bed (and she generally was). Didn't I know how hard Peter's illness had been on her, his own mother? I should be ashamed, a full-grown, able-bodied woman sleeping through the day.

I heard, but I couldn't respond. It was all I could do to drag myself out of bed once or twice a day to use the toilet, to drink a sip of milk from the carton and eat a spoonful of peanut butter from the jar, to splash cold water on my face, and then to collapse back into bed onto my belly, face mashed against the pillow. Peter's bear watched me sleep from the bedside table.

Worst of all were the dreams. I woke from them exhausted and sweating, often crying. Peter, a little boy again, lying on the ground, left leg bent under at a horrible angle, screaming my name over and over while I walked carelessly away. Peter with head and limbs in traction, unable to move, thirsty, dying of thirst, his water glass and straw sitting uselessly on his bedside table within inches of his head, while I stood with my back to him and looked out the window. Peter in bed, watching me approach, expecting his nightly syringe but then seeing the knife in my hands.

After I lay in bed for a couple of months, my mother finally called Dr. Halate and was happy to leave us alone together. I'm sure she hoped

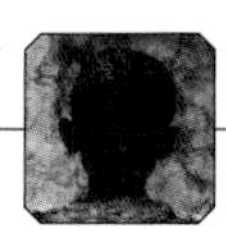

that Dr. Halate's pep talk would be more effective than hers in galvanizing me into action.

I apologized. "I don't know what's wrong. I'm not really ill. I just seem to have no energy."

"Sadness is the worst disease of all."

"And I have these dreams."

"Of course. Peter is lonely. He wants you."

"Perhaps I should just go, then."

"No. That would be a bad death. It wouldn't be your own."

"Are you saying that Peter's was a good death?"

"Yes. Don't you know that?"

I closed my eyes and let that knowledge wash over me. Then I said, "What should I do?"

"Good dreams should be kept, just as all other good things should be kept. But bad dreams must be sent away. You must tell them."

"I should tell you my dreams?"

"No. I'm not powerful enough to withstand them. I'll bring you something to help."

It turned out to be a one-inch-long piece of bluish-white bone. "This is the fossilized upper jaw of an ancient marmot," said Dr. Halate. "She once lived in a cave in Potosi Mountain in Nevada. Her jaw soaked for thousands of years in copper-rich water, changing the enamel of her teeth into pure turquoise."

Although the carved bear and the marmot's fossilized jaw were both stone, they were very different. Whereas the bear was rounded and smoothed and polished, the marmot's jaw was jagged and uneven, a sharp thing whose roughness contrasted astonishingly with the shining, bright blue teeth embedded in the jaw.

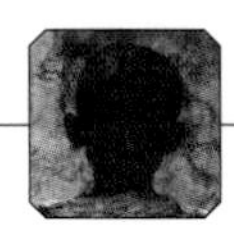

I asked, "How do you know this marmot was a female?" Dr. Halate shrugged.

I examined the jaw, running my fingers over the clashing textures of rough bone and smooth turquoise teeth, amazed at the vividness of that blue. "This is a wonderful color."

"Where I come from, that's the most important color. The sky is that color almost every day of the year, and it takes up most of your field of view. There are no trees, no tall buildings. Just that blue held up by the mountains. In that place, you will look up, not down."

She didn't say, "In that place, you look up." I remember she said, "In that place, you will look up." I thought about the whitish, grayish, mucus-colored sky over Trenton.

"Is this marmot more powerful than Peter's bear?"

"For you, yes. Tell her the bad dreams."

Dr. Weisman has finished his speech, the listeners have applauded, and now everyone is standing and stretching, ready for the main event of the evening: the unveiling of the new exhibit of Peter's skeleton, donated to the medical museum to advance the study of FOP disease in the hope of developing a cure. I'm a bit apprehensive about seeing my brother again after all this time, but I need to know that he's all right.

In the new bone pathology exhibit, I first see other skeletons, those who are now Peter's companions: A giant, a man who grew to be seven and a half feet tall. A dwarf, a woman who died in childbirth when her infant's head proved too big to pass through the birth canal. A humped-over woman with Pott's disease, spinal tuberculosis. All these people died in their twenties, as did Peter.

And then I see him. Even though I haven't seen him for years (and I never saw him like this), I recognize him immediately. He's standing in a glass case all by himself, illuminated by several small spotlights, the

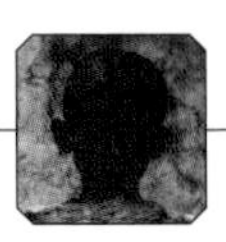

only skeleton who isn't held together at the joints with wires and pins. He is one piece, an entirety, a sculpture of bone. Sheets of leaf-thin bone cascade over his ribcage, fore and aft. His left elbow, wrist, and finger joints are encased in delicate bone sheaths. Stalactites of bone drip over his shoulder blades and collarbones.

He looks powerful. His nightmares and his agony have disappeared into history. Stripped of the painful flesh and the screeching nerves, he is inviolate now. I walk around the case, marveling. The boy of bone, my brother. He shines in the light, the paper-thin sheets of secondary bone bright white against the yellowish bone of the primary skeleton. He is the most brilliant thing in the room.

While the other guests listen to Dr. Weisman talk about Peter's generosity in donating his body for medical research, I walk around to the back of the case and kneel on the carpeted floor. There, on the bottom of Peter's exhibit case, just where the curator had assured me it would be, is Peter's bear, holding his iridescent fish, joyfully dancing in his stone eternity. I use the magnifying glass, the one I always carry in my purse now (along with the marmot's jaw), to read the label: "Fossil stone bear with coral eyes and abalone fish. Carved by unknown Zuni artist. Given by Dr. Helen Halate to Peter Dunstan in 1974. Displayed with skeleton at the request of the Dunstan family."

Getting up off the floor is not easy—my knees are not what they used to be—but I manage. A few of the guests are heading away from the exhibit, toward the table with the drinks and canapés, and a few others are talking among themselves or to Dr. Weisman. But most are inspecting Peter's skeleton, exclaiming in amazement and delight at its revelations. I hear someone say, "Penn researchers just announced that they've discovered the gene mutation that causes it."

They are speaking a language I no longer need to hear, so, after looking around to make sure I won't be intercepted, I duck into a nearby stairwell and escape the building through a side exit to catch a taxi to the airport.

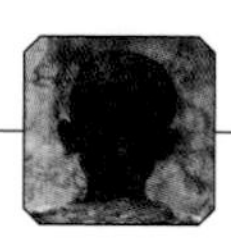

On the plane, I think about what I want to do when I get home. I've lived in New Mexico for nearly thirty years now. With the money from the sale of my mother's house, which I inherited after her death, I bought an old prospector's shack in the foothills of the Sandia Mountains north of Albuquerque. Learning as I went along, using the locals as sources of information and supplies and doing most of the work myself, I renovated that shack and improved its road to the highway, then sold it to a pair of snowbirds as their winter ski getaway. With the profit, I bought a couple of other shacks and did the same thing. Eventually, I earned enough to buy a trading post business with a shop, a house, and several artisans' studios on the land. The locals helped me renovate these buildings as well. I spent many, many hot days under the blazing blue sky, forming hundreds of adobe bricks by hand, sweat soaking my hair but evaporating instantly from my skin, heat baking me all the way through my bones. There is no stiffness in such heat; you feel melted.

I don't do hard physical labor like that anymore, of course. In fact, I don't do much work of any kind anymore. The shop managers do the trading and selling, the concession people furnish the cold drinks on the hot days, the artisans create their pots and baskets and stone carvings, the locals and the tourists come and go without paying much attention to me. When I feel like it, I walk around the place, looking at the artworks and chatting with people. I see some old Anglos like me, leather-brown skin spotted by the sun, gray hair pulled tightly back into thin rat-tails that snake down their backs. I meet a lot of Hispanic folks, and I talk to them in Spanglish, *en pochismo*. And I love meeting the people from the pueblos. I've learned some of their real (non-Spanish) names: Haaku rather than Acoma, Nafiathe rather than Sandia, Katishya rather than San Felipe. The Zia people keep their real name secret from outsiders, so I will probably never know it. I've asked a few of the Zuni if they know

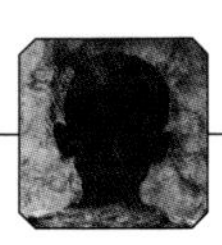

Dr. Helen Halate, but they say no. This no doesn't necessarily mean no, but I don't ask the same person twice.

No one needs me now except my two dusty old dogs. When I get home, I will sit with them on my front porch and look up at the brilliant turquoise sky.

FREDDY CHENG'S LIVE-DIE MUSEUM RESTAURANT

Hollywood, 2020, Chinese Lunar Year 4718, Year of the Rat

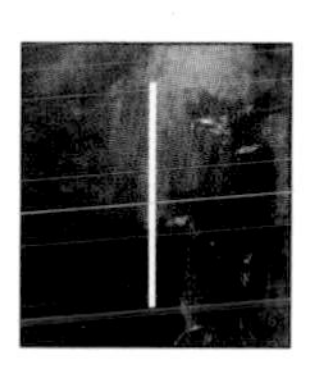

live near Hollywood, the great death-killer, the creator of bigger-than-life life, livelier-than-life life, truer-than-life life, every kind of life you can imagine and mostly kinds you can't, but no kind of death except the temporary kind, the weak kind, the pussy kind, where the guy who dies lives again for another film or award ceremony or else is just somebody who doesn't matter, like a director or a producer, somebody the Hollywood types pretend to mourn but who's really nobody at all. You know, like me and you, nobody who matters, nobody whose on-screen death serves the great purpose, which is to show once again (because you can't see it too many times) that death is a fiction, Hollywood's way of seducing us riffraff into forgetting about the floods and earthquakes and mudslides and brushfires that kill our houses and businesses and cars and animals every year, Hollywood's way of giving me enough time to toss my popcorn bag and drive to Diane's to get laid and then home to crash before dragging myself out of bed at the crack of doom. I got to get out to the curb to be picked up by Bigjohn as he swings the truck by to take us to

yet another trashed-out dead building (or pretend-dead, because after we clean it up and out, it'll come to life again as some new, better-than-ever-before, you-can't-imagine-how-much-you-need-this business), where we earn our pesos sorting real life's garbage into containers because some city ordinance says they can fine the crap out of you if you trash so much as one spitwad that could have been recycled or redbagged as biomedwaste.

Bigjohn isn't surprised we got the call for this job, because the restaurant's been closed for over two weeks, and our card was probably the only cleanout service in the Rolodex because Bigjohn was a friend of Freddy, the guy who owned the place, but before I tell the rest, I want you to know that Bigjohn isn't called that because he's bigger than me—in fact he's an inch or two shorter—but because he's older, and there's some weird psychology thing going on there, where you get somehow "bigger" with each birthday, and this is supposed to be some kind of compensation for getting older, because as far as I can tell there ain't any others.

Bigjohn and me have been working together a long time, get along pretty well, mostly I do the talking, he'd say that's because I don't know when to keep my mouth shut, I'd say it's because I got more to talk about because his life is too damn quiet. He just works, eats, and sleeps, never goes to clubs or bars, says he'd rather read books, and he never goes with women that I know of, still sore after Ellen left. He did try to help her, I know that, tried to keep the marriage going, kept working, kept putting food on the table, kept fucking her—he calls it "loving"—everything he'd done before that had been enough to keep them together. But after the baby died, those things all of a sudden weren't enough because Ellen said she needed him to share the grief, but he didn't know what that meant, and I don't blame him. Stupid idea, "sharing" grief like it was a piece of pie and if he took some there'd be less for her, but that don't make sense because two sad people instead of one sounds like double grief to me, not half grief. Anyway what was he supposed to do? Fall apart, cry big tears, hide under the covers like she did? Then pretty soon there wouldn't have been any covers or any roof or any food, and it would've been just the

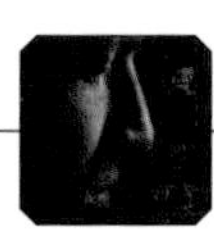

two of them curled up and wailing away, feeling worse and worse because not only would their kid still be dead but they'd be cold and hungry and homeless besides.

For today's job Bigjohn brings a lot more redbags than usual because the place to be cleaned out is a defunct theme restaurant that has a lot of medical specimens decorating it. I hear you ask Johnny? Medical specimens? What kind of decor is that for a restaurant? Well it was this real edgy upscale place for the past several years until the owner Freddy died, and then his brother, who didn't want anything to do with a restaurant decorated with medical specimens, ordered it cleared out, said get it ready to sell. I hear you ask Johnny? Where'd the specimens come from? Well Bigjohn says they came from some ancient medical museum on the East Coast where the bigwigs decided to go virtual, with bright clean touch-screens and lots of 2D and text, so they sent their old oil paintings to the nearest art museum and their medical instruments somewhere else, and they decided to dump the actual smelly decaying human body parts, which are very expensive to maintain, not to mention the impossible-to-please museum staff who kept whining about temperature controls and please-don't-touch and whatnot, so they fired the staff—I'm sure the bigwigs got a kick out of that—and auctioned the specimens off.

So the winning bidder was this Freddy guy who trucked the specimens across the country here to Hollywood and stuck them around his restaurant and served food in the shapes of them, you know hands and hearts and tits and so on (now I'm getting hungry), and got to be a celebrity, and people came from all around the world to eat his body-part-shaped food and have their pictures taken with him and his specimens, like the Beijing Globetrotters, who had themselves photographed with his skeleton of a giant, seven and a half feet tall, but even so, that giant is shorter than a couple of those Chinos, and yeah, everybody says they must be juiced, but the Chinese government claims it's just superior nutrition. Then there was that bunch of Chinese astronauts who were famous for about twenty seconds after they set up that lunar base,

who had themselves photographed with the specimen of the giant colon, a ginormous gut holding forty pounds of shit, I guess because they've finally conquered the problem of what to do with the astronauts' shit in space—apparently crapping in a nogravity environment has always been this tricky problem that NASA's kept hushhush—although when I asked Bigjohn why they didn't just put poopchutes in their spacecraft, he said it was because they'd all be sucked out into space along with their shit, and I said what a way to die and we both laughed, and he said see, Johnny? Our job ain't so bad after all.

So now we're driving along to this job, and I'm thinking about what Bigjohn told me about his kid's death and how it made Ellen feel worse when people said stupid things, like that she and he were lucky that the kid hadn't suffered, or that they were still young and could just have another one, or that God had wanted the dead kid for an angel or some bullshit like that, and Ellen would be forced to smile and say thanks before turning away to start crying all over again, refusing to take her happy pills and tranks, like she wanted to feel the hurt as much as possible because that's all that was left of their baby, just the hurt, and she was by God not going to give it up. Bigjohn said the worst thing about crib death is that there's no good answer to why—no virus, no faulty DNA, no drunk driver, no reason at all—so the answer to why is why not, and that's a damn crappy answer when it's your own kid's death you're asking about.

So now I'm riding along thinking about death, and I realize that for me death has always just meant gone or invisible, but at the same time a lot of invisible things aren't dead, like Australia, which I've never seen and probably never will, but I know it's out there somewhere, certainly not dead, not like Mom's brother Michael, gunned down in his school yard when he was only thirteen or so, and I've always thought of him as dead, but now I'm getting confused about what that actually means because let's say Michael was alive but in Australia, he'd be just as invisible as he is now, so what would be the difference? It would just be that Mom would get messages from him, but then again maybe not. What if he was alive

and living in Australia but just didn't want to talk to her? Lots of brothers and sisters get like that after their parents die and there's nothing else to hold them together, so being dead could be just the same thing as living in Australia but not wanting to talk.

Bigjohn said he started eating at the Live-Die Museum Restaurant after Ellen left, because he was sick of his own cooking and his own sadness, and he needed people around who didn't know about Ellen and Adam, people who thought he was just a regular hungry customer, and he'd never been there with her, so it'd be a fresh start, and that was right around the time Freddy brought in the specimens and started putting them around the place, and I hear you ask Johnny? How come such a weird thing caught on? Yeah, that's definitely hard to say because in theory people shouldn't want to eat in a restaurant decorated with parts of human corpses and models of human biological systems, but the crowds rolled in, and it seemed to be more than just because everyone was doing it or because it was a new thing. Bigjohn thinks maybe it was a kind of victory, a celebration that they were still alive as in *I eat therefore I am*. Anyway he always sat with the babies in the jars, and of course none of them was his baby, but that was okay because those babies' parents were gone just like his baby was gone, so they were all kind of in the same boat together, and maybe it wasn't as good as being with your own folks, but it was a helluva lot better than being with nobody.

So after Bigjohn and I arrive at the Live-Die, we find that the place isn't as much of a mess as we feared, the worst smells coming from the spoiled food in the kitchen, not from the parts of the dead people that we walk around looking at, even though I can't really make them click as something that was once alive because they look like the movie props I saw that time I took the Warner Brothers tour and saw props from the dozen or so *Matrix* films and the twenty or so *Harry Potter* films, and I have only Bigjohn's word that these body parts are real, but he also shows me some things that really are props, not parts, like the wax mask of an old woman with a horn, and I say what's up with that? And he says well

it's just a model, but I'm showing it to you so you know you don't have to redbag it thinking it's biomedwaste when it's actually just trash, so I trash it and move on to the next several thousand things.

And so I'm shoveling up all the paper for recycling, and I see a real old photograph that I recognize from a book I read in school a long time ago about Lincoln's assassination, a photo that shows four people hanging with their feet tied together and hoods on their heads and armed soldiers looking on, and one of the four is wearing a dress, and now I remember that this was the first woman ordered to be executed by the United States government, and I'm marveling at how I haven't thought about this woman for years, but there she is and I recognize her right away, and I wonder if that six degrees of separation thing that up till now I thought just applied to living people maybe includes dead ones as well, which would open up a whole new world of possibilities.

And while I'm shoveling paper, Bigjohn's telling me that he always used to get a kick out of the reaction of new customers to the menu, because although the Live-Die offered only vegetarian food, apparently this guy Freddy was a real master of presentation. Like for instance his potstickers didn't have any pork in them at all, just tofu, but once he mixed it all up with everything else—you know, carrots, bok choy, bamboo shoots, garlic, chives, sesame oil, and all the other stuff—no one could tell that the pork was missing, because the taste and the texture were perfect, like really tender pork with no gristly bits at all. So once the customers got into the swing of things they'd order up food in the shapes of their favorite specimens, like amputated legs and arms, kind of like how they do at that old mission San Xavier del Bac, where people offer up miniature models of body parts, milagros, as prayers when they need healing, like for instance if they're worried about going blind, they light a candle and offer a little pair of eyes to let Jesus know what he needs to be paying attention to, so I guess it was something like that going on here at the Live-Die. Bigjohn says if you can't figure out why something's happening, you need to dig deeper into human psychology,

so I ask Bigjohn if, when he ate here at the Live-Die, he used to eat food shaped like babies, and he smiled and said sure, and I asked did it make him feel better? And he said of course, nothing could hurt his baby once it was safe inside him, and that made sense in a weird kind of way.

So I'm shoveling away at the paper, and now I see right on top of the next load another real old photograph, again a woman but this one is naked, and my response to it surprises me because it's the first time I can remember getting hard because of a woman's color. I've never cared about brown, yellow, red, black, or white—in fact a green one would be fine as long as she's naked and smiling—I love that pillowy, mattressy feeling that invites me to sink down, sink in, forget my troubles, and that yeasty smell that comes after I've been at her awhile, like I'm a loaf of bread and she's my oven, and afterward, when my whole body feels stretched and melted and relaxed, it's the greatest feeling in the world. The guys who lay on me their two cents about skin color and cultural purity and racial loyalty and say I should just go with brown ladies, well I just laugh at them and say hell, I want to fuck a woman, not a culture or a race. Absolutely nothing wrong with Diane, and she ain't brown as far as I can see; actually I'm not sure what all she is—maybe she don't even know herself—and the subject's never come up because we've got better things to do together than give each other the third degree about our DNA.

So my reaction to this photograph is weird because I find myself moved by this woman's whiteness, specifically by her white ass because she's lying on her side on a cloth-covered table, ass to the camera, head turned away and resting on a fancy fringed pillow, face hidden, hair done up on top of her head in some kind of frizzy mess, and her ass isn't enormous—she's a small woman everywhere—but it's really white against the darkness of the tablecloth and the wall, like a bright moon on a black night, and I can't help staring at it. Her legs are stretched out knock-kneed, causing the space between her ass cheeks to open up just enough for me to see inside a bit, to get the dark outline in there, and just that subtle hint of sex stirs me more than if she was showing me everything

she had, and I yell hey, what's so medical about this? And Bigjohn comes over and looks at it and smiles and says he don't know, and when I say I need to take a break, he laughs in that unh-huh way that shows he thinks I'm off to the toilet to jiggle the old johnson, and of course he's right, that's exactly what I mean to do.

But once I get there and look at her some more, I get distracted and start wondering when the photo was taken and why and who she was and why she did let somebody take a picture of her like that, and then I realize my hardon's gone, and I get a little panicky and run out and yell for Bigjohn because I'm afraid something's wrong with me, but he just smiles and says good for you, Johnny, you're growing up, and so we look at her some more and decide that she was pretty young, maybe fifteen or so, probably some starving Irish immigrant who needed the money so she posed, and we both sure as hell understand about doing shit we don't like because we need the money. I think about pocketing the photo, but I don't want to take a chance on hurting Diane if she finds it, and anyway it don't seem right now that the girl in the photo has become a real person in my mind, so I lay the photo gently on top of the ton of paper already in the recycling bin, and Bigjohn nods and smiles but don't say nothing.

So we break to eat, and afterward Bigjohn comes over with a question about something he's found, a little head with longlong black hair that looks sort of human but neither of us is sure, and Bigjohn thinks it might be a real shrunken head for the biomedwaste redbag, but I think it's just a model because no human head could be that small (not even baby Adam's), so the two of us have to decide, but since we can't agree on what it is, we agree that the safest course of action is the redbag option, when in doubt and the lesser of two weevils and all that. But when it comes right down to it I just don't want to admit this thing might actually be a human head because that would mean it used to hold a brain and eyes and tongue and used to be attached to a body that grew inside a woman and then came out as a baby and was fed and cared for as he grew and was loved, at least I hope so, and then he learned to run and talk and

lots of other stuff, and maybe he lived long enough to travel around a bit and get laid a few times, but then some asshole came along and cut off his head and shrunk it, and ever since then his head has been kicking around the world not getting the respect that the dead should get, so if it really is a human head, it's high damn time for it to be laid to rest.

But then I start to feel bad because I don't want to be the one to destroy the head after it's been around for so long, maybe even over a hundred years, so Bigjohn says well, Johnny, nothing's ever really destroyed. This head'll just change shape inside the incinerator, separate into molecules of copper and oxygen and other stuff, and all those molecules will move out into the air and the earth and the water, and they'll become parts of other things like plants and bugs that ducks eat, or like air that dogs breathe, or like diamonds which are made out of carbon same as people. So this head won't ever really be gone, and neither will anything else.

So then I feel better, and I redbag the head, and we go on working until two-three in the morning, better to get the thing over with than to have to come back, and the place is looking pretty good now, and the brother of the dead restaurant owner won't have nothing much to do before he puts it up for sale besides just a paint job and maybe new flooring and lights, so we haul out the last of the trash and close up all the dumpsters. We're stretching and yawning and drinking coffee before it's time to get into the truck, and all of a sudden Bigjohn looks up and says hey Johnny! An eclipse! And I look up to see the moon is a nasty brownish-red color like dried blood, very spooky, and I see why those people in the past got afraid because it's definitely ugly, especially when that last white sliver goes, and the whole moon is murky and wounded-looking. But then Bigjohn reminds me that those Chinese astronauts on the moon must be watching from over there at this very second, watching the earth being eclipsed, and that's a very cool thing to think about, those guys and us looking at the same thing at the same time even though we're a couple hundred thousand miles apart. And then Bigjohn points out something I'd never noticed, which is that when the moon's gone dark,

the stars that are right near it are visible so you can actually watch the moon move across them, and this is something you can't do when the moon is too bright for you to see those stars so close to it, so even the murky bloodiness of the eclipsed moon has a silver lining. So we watch the moon move across those new stars for a while, something I've never seen before, so it's pretty interesting, but then after a while a white sliver shows up on the opposite side of where the last sliver disappeared, and we see that the moon's coming back to its normal self, like it always does. The darkness is always just temporary, but even when it's dark you can see something new and amazing if you look for it.

ACKNOWLEDGMENTS

Many people helped this book along with encouragement, information, or both. Helen W. Mallon, my writing coach, taught me that implication trumps explication (in fiction, at least). Anna Dhody, curator of the Mütter Museum of the College of Physicians of Philadelphia, shared her amazing knowledge of human anatomy so I could better understand the machine that houses the ghost. Evi Numen, exhibitions manager for the same museum, used her unlimited vision to show me how to see human bodies in a larger way. Annie Brogan, librarian for the Historical Medical Library of the College of Physicians of Philadelphia, fed my indiscriminate bibliophilia with her own. My brother John Davis, my sister Margaret Burton, and my friend Barbara Hamilton read early drafts of these stories and cheered me on. Gina Ochsner, a dream writer of color and flight, was most generous with her compliments. Janine Armin, David Duhr, Seth Jani, Suzanne Kamata, Robert Scott Leyse, Chris Lynch, Caleb Mathern, Mitch Parker, Sophie Playle, Cynthia Reeser, Forrest Roth, and Mike Wever were the journal and anthology editors who accepted some of these stories for initial publication. George Wohlreich, director of the College of Physicians of Philadelphia, insisted that I find a publisher for this collection. Ken Siman kindly (and perhaps recklessly) offered to be that publisher. Jon Lezinsky and Jason Snyder made this book beautiful to the eye. Ann Espuelas and Anna Jardine edited the text with wonderful rigor. And Robert Hicks, director of the Mütter Museum and Medical Historical Library of the College of Physicians of Philadelphia, whose unflagging delight in these stories was my best incentive to keep writing them, proved yet again that marrying him was the smartest thing I ever did.

ABOUT THE AUTHOR

K.R. Sands has worked as a zookeeper, animal laboratory technician, English professor, and government policy analyst. She has a Ph.D. in English literature and the history of ideas from the University of Arizona. This is her first book of fiction.